Fundamentals of Nintex Workflow for SharePoint 2013

Michael B McManus

Trademark Notice

PowerPoint, Windows, Word, Microsoft, and SharePoint are trademarks of Microsoft, Inc. Throughout this courseware title, trademark names are used. Nintex is a trademark of Nintex. Rather than put a trademark symbol in each occurrence of a trademarked name, we state we are using the names only in an editorial fashion and to the benefit of the trademark owner with no intention of infringement of the trademark.

Disclaimer

We make a sincere effort to ensure the accuracy of the material described herein; however the author makes no warranty, expressed or implied, with respect to the quality, correctness, reliability, accuracy, or freedom from error of this document or the products it describes. Data used in examples and sample data files are intended to be fictional. Any resemblance to real persons or companies is entirely coincidental. Sample materials including lab samples, data files, product specifications, tables etc. may include materials from publicly available sources such as Nintex.com, Product help files, MSDN, TechNet, jQuery.com etc.

Nintex Workflow for SharePoint 2013

What is Workflow?

What is a workflow? Some might define a workflow as being process automation. This is correct, but a workflow in a SharePoint site can be much more. Essentially a workflow can be as simple as automatically sending an email to someone if a document is uploaded, or automatically updating a column value based upon some user interaction; or a workflow can be very complicated, involving multiple SharePoint lists, libraries and users.

Online versus On - Premises

Nintex Workflows for SharePoint 2013 can be used to develop workflows for either On-Premises SharePoint and for SharePoint Online (Office 365). Building workflows in either On-Premises SharePoint or SharePoint Online follows the same process - using the Nintex Workflow Designer to build workflows using Workflow Actions. The primary difference between Nintex Workflow for SharePoint On-Premises versus Nintex Workflow for SharePoint Online (Office 365) is the available Workflow Actions. For the most part both versions of Nintex Workflow for SharePoint 2013 have the same Workflow Actions, but some are different - some Workflow Actions are available in the On-Premises version which are not available in the SharePoint Online version - and vice versa.

In both Nintex Workflow for SharePoint 2013 On-Premises and SharePoint Online workflows are build using online tools - no client tools are needed.

In most cases this book will use the Nintex Workflow for SharePoint 2013 On-Premises version for screen shots, but will highlight differences between the two versions and will clearly identify screenshots from the SharePoint Online (Office 365) version.

Steps to Building a Nintex Workflow

A Nintex Workflow is built using 6 basic steps:

- Define the Workflow Name
- Define the Workflow Initiation Options (how will the workflow start)
- Define the Workflow layout (what Workflow Actions will be needed)
- Define any needed Workflow Variables
- Configure Workflow Actions
- Publish the Workflow

Types of Nintex Workflows

Nintex Workflows for SharePoint 2013 are built and published either to a specific SharePoint List (or Library), to a SharePoint Content Type, or to a SharePoint Site.

List and Library Workflows

SharePoint 2013 List and Library Nintex Workflows are associated with one specific SharePoint list or one specific SharePoint library. List and Library Nintex Workflows are created and managed from the list or library the workflow will be used for - via the list or library ribbon. List and Library Nintex Workflows are not re-usable.

Create Site Workflow

Manage Site Workflows

View Workflow History

Schedule Site Workflows

Create Reusable Workflow Template

Manage Reusable Workflow Templates

Create Site Collection Reusable Workflow Template

Manage Site Collection Reusable Workflow Templates

Manage User Defined Actions

List and Library workflows have an item context. In other words because a Nintex Workflow for a list or library is associated with a specific list or library the workflow, while running, is aware of the list and list item the workflow is running on. For this reason when configuring workflow actions for a List or Library workflow the workflow provides us with a *Current Item* selector.

List and Library Nintex Workflows can be started manually or automatically when an item in the list or library is either created or modified.

Re-Usable Workflows (Content Type Workflow)

Re-Usable Nintex Workflows are not associated with a specific SharePoint list or a specific SharePoint library; rather they are associated with a SharePoint Content Type. Once a re-usable Nintex Workflow has been created it can be used by any list or library with the associated SharePoint Content Type.

Re-Usable Nintex Workflows can be created and published for either a single SharePoint Web (single SharePoint site) or a SharePoint Site Collection. The only difference is the scope - will the workflow be available to all sites within the Site Collection or will it only be available for the current Site.

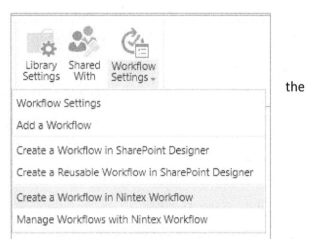

Re-Usable Nintex Workflows have an item context. In other words because a Re-Usable Nintex Workflow is associated with lists or libraries the workflow, while running, is aware of the list and list item the workflow is running on. For this reason when configuring workflow actions for a List or Library workflow the workflow provides us with a *Current Item* selector.

Re-Usable Nintex Workflows are only available in On-Premises Nintex Workflow for SharePoint 2013. They are not available in Nintex Workflow for SharePoint Online (Office 365).

Re-Usable Nintex Workflows can be started manually or automatically when an item in the list or library is either created or modified.

Site Workflows

Nintex Site Workflows are not associated with specific lists or libraries. Site workflows run without a specific list or item context, and therefore cannot be started automatically based upon a list item being added or modified. Site Workflows however can be scheduled to run. Site workflows are very useful for utility type automation - execute some action on selected lists every night for example.

Enterprise Features

Installing an Enterprise license for Nintex Workflow 2013 provides additional functionality - the enterprise features are optional for on-premises Nintex Workflow for SharePoint 2013 - Nintex Workflow for Office 365 provides full functionality without choosing an Enterprise option.

The following additional Workflow features are provided by the Enterprise license (the following is from the NINTEX FOR WORKFLOW 2013 EDITION COMPARISON document):

Active Directory Account Provisioning

Workflow actions to support automated provisioning tasks such as: adding/removing users to/from Active Directory (AD) groups; creating, updating, and decommissioning Active Directory accounts.

Exchange Server Mailbox Provisioning

Create and remove Exchange Server (2003, 2007, 2010 and 2013) mailbox privileges for Active Directory accounts.

Lync/OCS Privilege Provisioning

Enabling/disabling Microsoft Lync Server (2010 and 2013, as well as Office Communication Server 2007) (Lync/OCS) privileges on Active Directory accounts.

User Profiles & Audiences

Workflow actions support add/update/delete operations on the SharePoint Server User Profile Store, including properties, Member Group, and memberships. Audiences can be created, deleted, modified, and recalculated.

Universal Workflow Inbox/Status

The two out of the box web parts, "My Workflow Tasks" and "Workflows I've Started" can be configured at a farm level, allowing users to refer to one location to track all workflows pertaining to them.

Workflow Reporting

Workflow statistics are available on each workflow providing a holistic view of workflow performance. This includes details on average run time, total runs, amount of workflows in progress, as well as user performance, making it a crucial feature to identify bottlenecks in business processes.

Reporting capabilities are further extended through data driven and graphical web parts including reports like 'average workflow completion time', 'standard variations', 'minimum and maximum completion times' and 'user response times'.

Exchange Server Integration

Workflow actions to create Outlook tasks and appointments and retrieve suggested meeting times.

For example, a leave approval workflow could add the approved leave to the applicant's and their manager's calendars. Because the Exchange Server web service APIs are used, this method is also suited to various on-premise, hosted, and hybrid architectures.

Search

Execute queries against SharePoint Server's enterprise search engine and incorporate the results into workflows. This works with both full-text and property based queries.

Business Data Connectivity

Nintex Workflow 2007 can query the SharePoint 2007 Business Data Catalog (BDC) to retrieve data from line of business applications and external databases. Nintex Workflow 2010 and 2013 can connect to SharePoint 2010 and 2013 Business Connectivity Services (BCS) respectively, to read and write data to external data sources.

SharePoint Records Management Integration

Workflows can submit documents to SharePoint Server record center sites, allowing for workflows to help manage content development throughout their entire life cycle, all with an easy user interface and with minimal complexity exposed to users.

Excel Services

Excel worksheet models can be executed and used by workflows. Excel Services for SharePoint Server can expose calculation models and spreadsheet data via a SOAP Web service. This workflow action makes it easy for users to provide inputs and read results from worksheets.

Word Services

Workflow actions to manipulate Word documents via Word Services. Allows server based document construction, form field updates, and document conversion to PDF and other formats.

BizTalk Server Integration

Enable interaction with BizTalk Server. The action can send messages into a BizTalk orchestration and/

or wait for a message from BizTalk Server. This action allows a workflow to interact with any external system that BizTalk Server interoperates with.

Microsoft Dynamics CRM Integration

Workflow actions to create, delete, and update data in Microsoft Dynamics CRM software.

The Nintex Workflow Designer

Nintex Workflows are build using the Nintex Workflow Designer to select, organize and configure Workflow Actions. Workflow Actions perform the steps and functions of the workflow. The Workflow Designer is the same in both the On-Premises and Online versions of Nintex Workflow for SharePoint 2013.

Nintex Workflow Designer Canvas

The Nintex Workflow Designer Canvas is a web based user interface which makes it very easy to lay out a workflow in a visual, easy to understand format. The Design Canvas is just that, a canvas. You build workflows by dragging workflow actions onto the canvas.

Note the pane of Workflow Actions on the left side of the screen and the open area in the center. The Green Arrow represents the start of the workflow and the Red Square represents the end of the workflow. Workflows are built by dragging workflow actions onto the bubble between the start and the stop. When a workflow action is added to the design canvas additional bubbles appear, indicating locations where additional workflow actions can be placed. In the screenshot below an Assign Flexi Task workflow action has been added between the workflow start and the workflow end. Now instead of one bubble there are 4 bubbles. This means additional workflow tasks can be added in 4 places within the workflow - above the Assign Flexi Task action (before the Assign Flexi Task action in the workflow sequence), below the Assign Flexi Task action (after the Assign Flexi Task action in the workflow sequence), inside the Reject branch and inside the Approve branch.

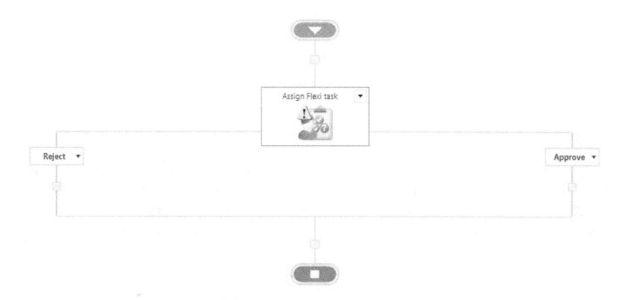

Workflows are built by dragging additional workflow actions onto the design canvas. The order and sequence of actions, and the configuration of the workflow actions are what really define the workflow's functionality or what the workflow does!

Ribbon Icons - List and Library Workflows

The SharePoint Ribbon is used to create, modify and delete Nintex Workflows for a specific list or library. Upon activating the Nintex Workflow for SharePoint 2013 Site Feature, the Out of the Box SharePoint 2013 List/Library ribbon adds two additional options to the Workflow Settings menu:

- Create a Workflow in Nintex Workflow

- Manage Workflows with Nintex Workflows

SharePoint 2013 On Premises presents Nintex Workflow menu items on the List or Library Ribbon as menu items of the Workflow Settings Ribbon icon as in the image below.

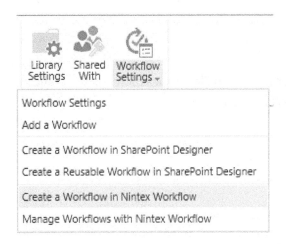

For SHAREPOINT 2013 ON PREMISES there is a menu option for creating a new Nintex Workflow (on the current list or library) and for managing Nintex Workflows (for the current list or library). The Manage Workflows with Nintex Workflow menu item is how you edit or delete existing Nintex Workflows. It is important to remember that these menu items are List/Library specific in terms of Nintex Workflows.

For NINTEX WORKFLOWS FOR OFFICE 365 (SharePoint Online) there is a separate icon for Nintex Workflows, it is not a sub menu of Workflow Settings. Note there is also only one option for Nintex Workflow, there is not a specific icon for Creating versus Managing workflows.

Clicking the Ninex Workflow icon opens the Nintex Workflow for Office 365 Design interface. The choice to create a new Ninex Workflow versus modify or delete an exisiting Nintex Workflow is handled by whether you click New or Open on the Nintex Workfow ribbon

The Site Settings (Site Actions) Nintex Menu

Nintex Workflows for SharePoint 2013 On Premises support Site Workflows and additional options within the Site Actions (Gear) menu. You will notice on a SharePoint site with the Nintex Workflow Site Feature Activated a Nintex Workflow 2013 sub menu is added to the SharePoint Site Actions (Gear) menu:

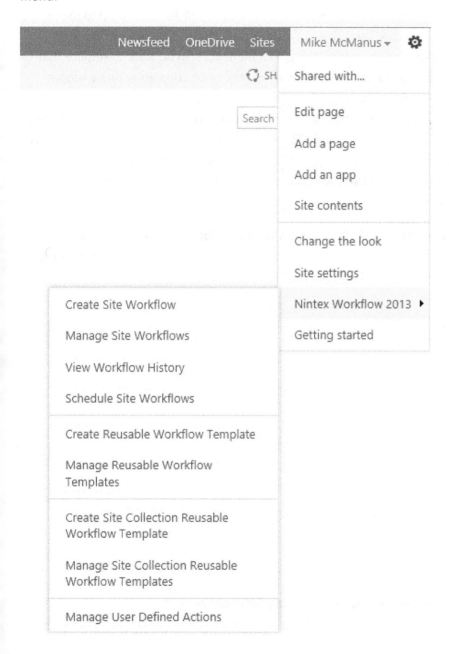

Using the Site Actions (Gear) menu provides easy access to a sub menu with commands for creating and managing Site Workflows, Reusable Workflows and User Defined Actions (UDAs).

Note this functionality is only available for SharePoint On Premises.

Task Driven Workflows

Workflows in SharePoint are Task Driven. This means that task items, in task lists, are used to manage many of the things being done by the workflow. Think of a simple workflow - an approval workflow. Whenever someone creates a new document in a selected document library you want to require that the author's supervisor approves or rejects the newly submitted document. Implementing a simple workflow would accomplish this very nicely, we would 'assign an approval task to the author's supervisor. How is this done? It is quite literally done by creating a task item in a task list and updating the Assigned To value to the author's supervisor (or manager in AD); and so while we don't think about document approval as something related to a SharePoint task list, the task list is necessary behind the scenes for SharePoint to keep track of things like the status of the Approval Request, are reminders necessary and if so when should they be sent out.

One of the most commonly used workflow actions in Nintex Workflow for SharePoint 2013 is the Assign a Flexi Task action. As seen below this action results in an outcome (such as Reject or Approve) and as the name implies it is based upon a task item (or workflow task item) content type.

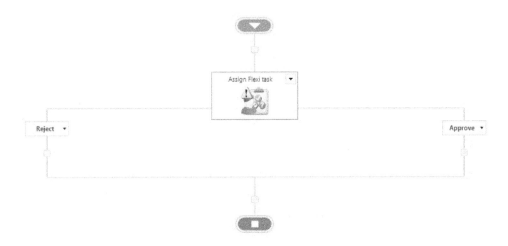

Is a task assignment like the Assign Flexi Task action necessary for every workflow?

No. Not at all. But you gain a lot with a task driven workflow. Let's look at a few demonstrations.

In the following demonstration we will see how a simple approval workflow can be implemented to enhance the standard out of the box Approval Process available on SharePoint lists and libraries. This demonstration will not use a task list. It will simply send an email to the supervisor (or other approver) to let them know there is an item awaiting their review and approval.

Demo 1 - Enhancing the out of the box Approval process
* This demo can be done in either on-premises SharePoint or Office 365 - SharePoint Online

The out of the box Approval process in SharePoint allows a site owner to indicate that content created or modified in a SharePoint list or library requires approval by a designated approver (someone with permissions to approve or reject content). Unfortunately the out of the box Approval process does not notify anyone that there is something awaiting review and approval.

In this demonstration we will add a simple email notification to alert all approvers about new content awaiting their review.

*Note - SharePoint comes with an out of the box workflow called the approval workflow which creates a review and approve task; and assigns the review and approval task to an approver. This out of the box workflow does include email notification. In this workflow we will only notify approvers and will not create a task.

- Start by creating an out of the box **Document Library**

- On the **Gear** icon in the upper right click **Add an App**

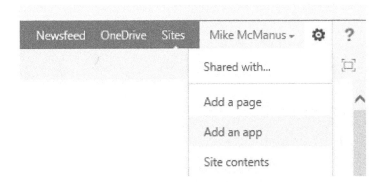

- On the **Your Apps** page click **Document Library** to create a new SharePoint list based on the **Document Library** template

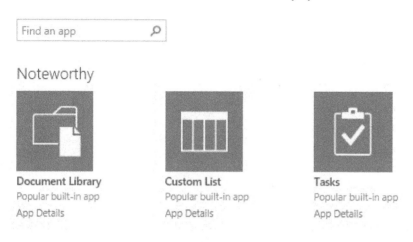

- Name the library as **YourName_WF_Documents** and click **Create**

- Once the new library has been created click on it on the **Site Contents** page to navigate to the library

- On the **Library** tab of the ribbon click **Library Settings**

- On the **Library Settings** page click **Versioning Settings**

Documents · Settings

List Information

Name: Documents

Web Address: http://dev.xspects.com

Description:

General Settings

- List name, description and navigation
- Versioning settings
- Advanced settings
- Validation settings
- Column default value settings
- Rating settings
- Audience targeting settings
- Form settings

- On the Versioning Settings page click Yes to Require content approval for submitted items

Settings · Versioning Settings

Content Approval

Specify whether new items or changes to existing items should remain in a draft state until they have been approved.   Learn about requiring approval.

Require content approval for submitted items?
⦿ Yes   ○ No

- Scroll down and click **OK**

The approval process is now set up. Look at the library and you will see the Approval Status column has been added

Documents

⊕ new document or drag files here

All Documents   Approve/reject Items   My submissions   •••

✓ ▢   Name   Modified   Modified By   Approval Status

There are no files in the view "All Documents".

- Add a document (just drag a file onto the 'drag files here' section of the page)

Documents

Upload completed (1 added)   DISMISS

All Documents   Approve/reject Items   My submissions   •••   Find a file   🔍

✓	🗋	Name	Modified	Modified By	Approval Status
	📄	Sample 1 ✿ •••	A few seconds ago	☐ Mike McManus	Pending

The Approval Status of the new document is 'Pending'. Someone with Approver permissions must take action to approve or reject the document, but unless an approver browses to the library and sees items with a 'Pending' status they will not know something is awaiting their review.

With a very simple workflow we can add a notification email to the process

- Click the dropdown on the **Workflow Settings** icon on the Library tab of the ribbon and click **Create a Workflow in Nintex Workflow**

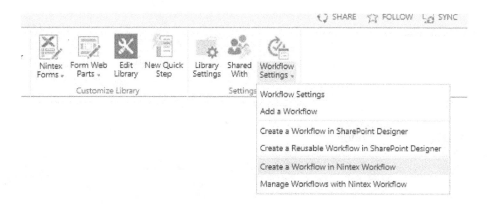

- When prompted to select a template choose a **Blank** template and click **Create**

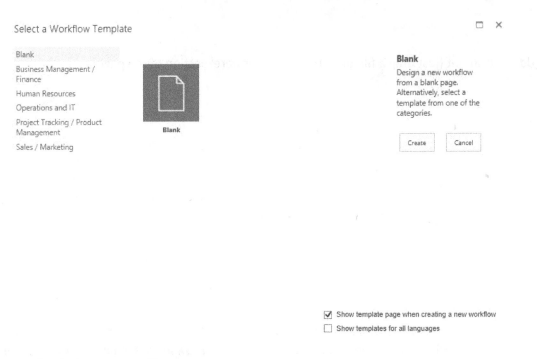

- The design canvas will open

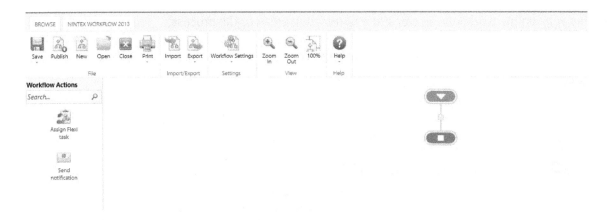

- Click **Workflow Settings** on the ribbon

- On the **Workflow Settings** page give the workflow a name and select **Yes** to **start when items are created**

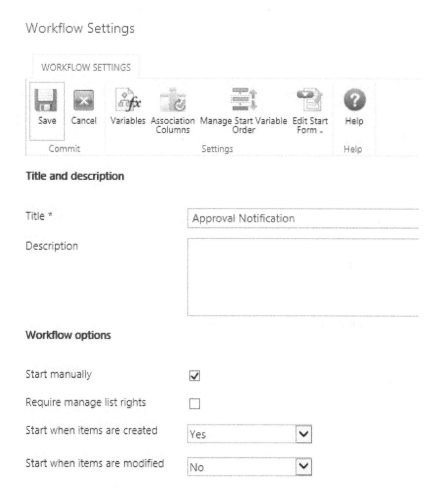

- **Save** the changes
- Because we only want to send an email for Pending approvals first drag a **Set a Condition** action onto the design canvas. The **Set a Condition** action is in the **Logic and Flow** section

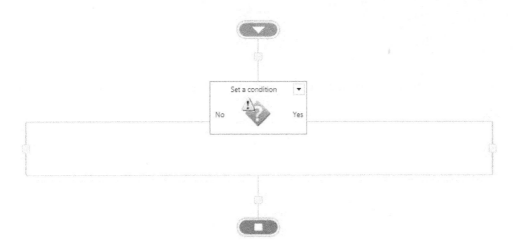

- Click the dropdown arrow in the upper right of the action to configure the action settings

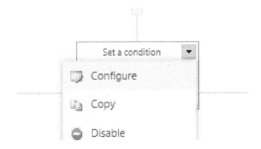

- Set the values on the **Condition** action as below and click **Save**

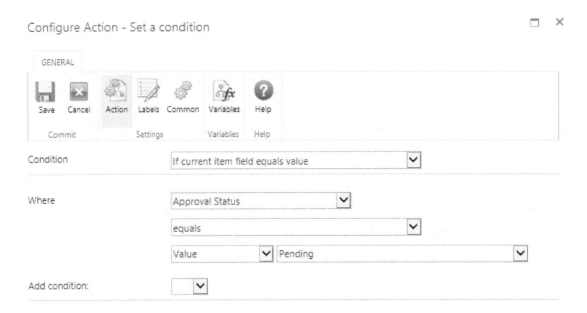

- The condition will evaluate to Yes if the Approval Status is Pending and will evaluate to No if the Approval Status is anything other than Pending which is why the design canvas has two paths

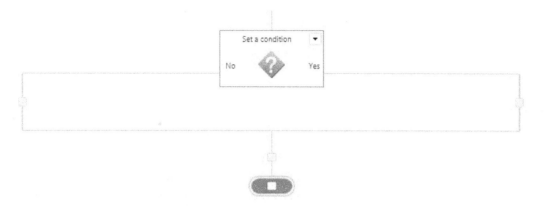

- We will only send an email notification when the condition evaluates to **True**, so we need to drag a **Send Notification** action onto the **Yes** path

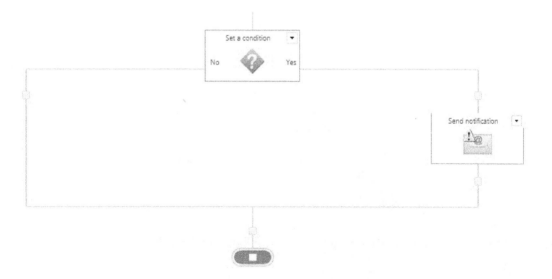

- Click the dropdown arrow on the upper right of the **Send notification** action to configure the action settings

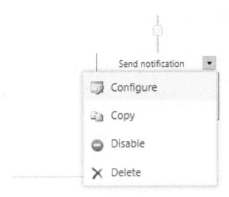

- On the **Configure Action** page click the address book icon to the right of the **To** field

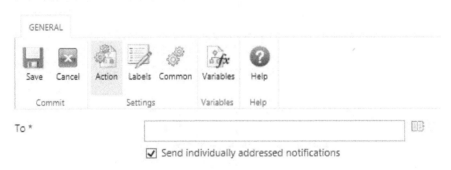

- On the **Select People and Groups** dialog click **Lookup** and then choose **Manager**

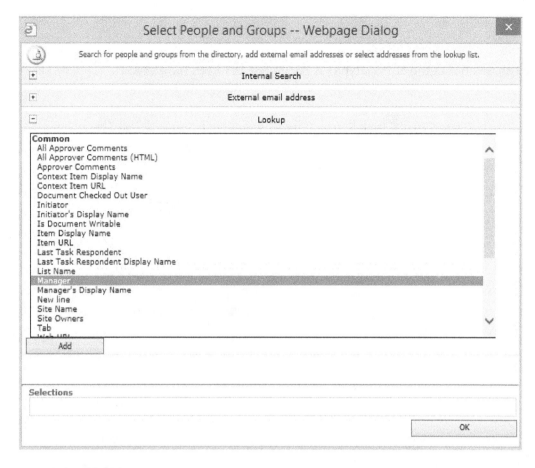

- Click **Add** and **OK**

- Enter **_A document requires your review_** as the email subject

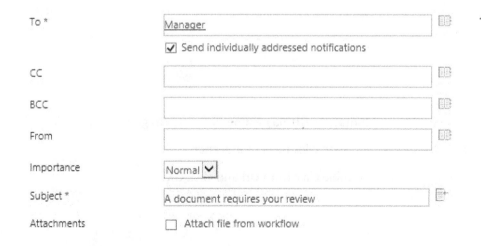

- In the rich text box at the bottom type - *A document has been submitted by* and then click **Insert Reference**

- On the Insert Reference page double click **Initator's Display Name** and click **OK**

- In the rich text box after the **Initiator's Display Name** hit return to go to the next line. Type *You can view this document at* and then click **Insert Reference**

- On the Insert Reference page double click **Item Url** and click **OK**

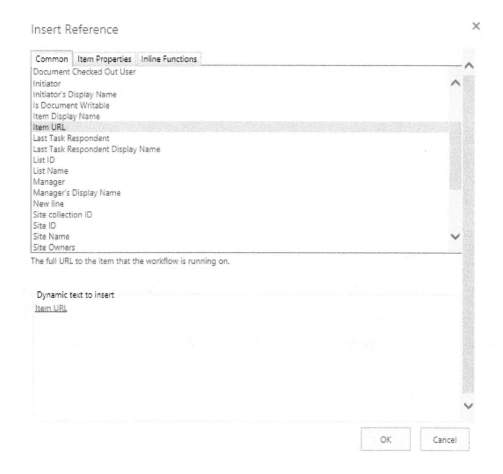

- Save the Notification Action configuration

- **Save** and **Publish** the workflow

- Add a new document to the Library. A new column should appear showing the status of the workflow

MikeM_WF_Documents

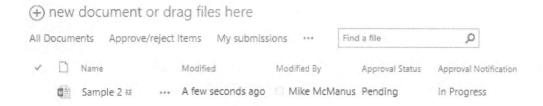

⊕ new document or drag files here

All Documents   Approve/reject Items   My submissions   •••   Find a file   🔎

✓	🗋 Name	Modified	Modified By	Approval Status	Approval Notification
	📄 Sample 2 ✖ •••	A few seconds ago	☐ Mike McManus	Pending	In Progress

- We can also review the status of the workflow. Click on the status - In Progress, Completed, etc.
- The Workflow Status page will open showing basic information about the workflow

- We can also see a visual depiction of the workflow which can be very helpful to track the progress on really long or complex workflows
- Using the ellipses for the document you uploaded click on **View Workflow History**

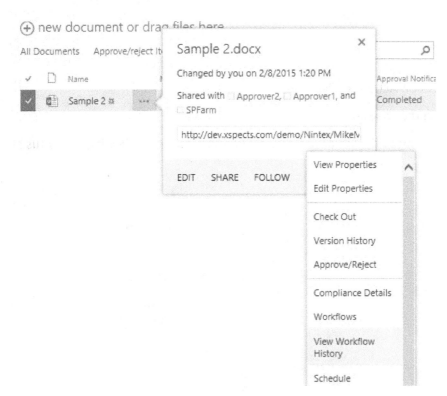

- Click the workflow instance you want to see

- This will open a visual depiction of the workflow. Note that both actions are green. This is because the workflow is complete, so we see a green path all the way from start to end. If the workflow was in progress, the actions that had not yet been completed would show as yellow

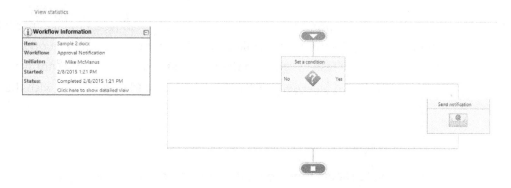

- If we click **Click here to show detailed view** it shows us:

The demonstration accomplishes the goal of alerting a manager that their attention is needed to review and approve/reject a new document. But what if the manager doesn't see the email? Or simply forgets about it? Or is out of the office for an extended time? By assigning an Approval Task to the manager rather than simply sending the manager an email asking them to review the content we can keep of track of whether the manager has completed the approval request. The Approval Task can also handle things like escalation - what to do if the task is not completed in a timely manner, or what to do if more than one approver is assigned.

The next demonstration shows these extra benefits obtained by using a task - such as the Assign Flexi Task.

Demo 2 - Using the Flexi Task Action

In the last demonstration we created a simple process to send an email to an employee's manager to let them know there was a document needing their review. While this simple notification model works fine, the best practice is to create a workflow task assigned to the Manager. Not only will this notify the Manager about a document needing review, it will keep track of if or when the Manager deals with the assigned review.

The flexi task workflow action is unique to Nintex Workflows, it is used instead of the standard SharePoint task item.

The Flexi Task is only available with on-premises SharePoint

- Click the dropdown on the **Workflow Settings** icon on the Library tab of the ribbon and click **Create a Workflow in Nintex Workflow**

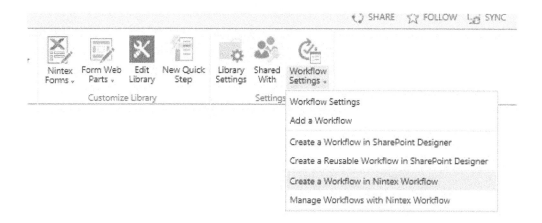

- When prompted to select a template choose a **Blank** template and click **Create**

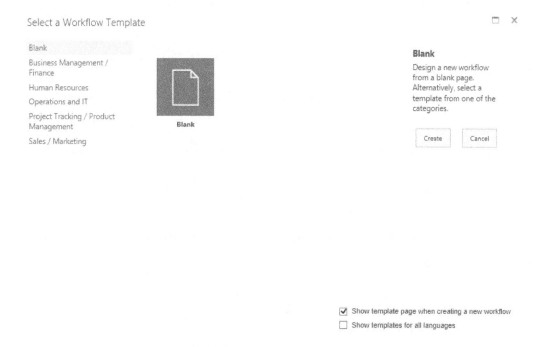

- The design canvas will open

- Click **Workflow Settings** on the ribbon

- On the **Workflow Settings** page give the workflow a name and select **Yes** to **start when items are created**. Click **Save**

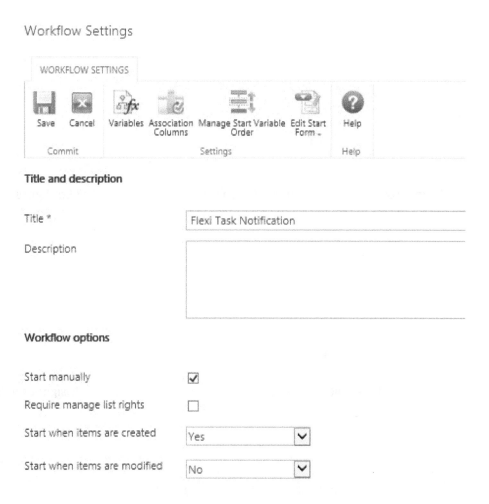

- Drag a **Flexi Task** action onto the canvas. Note that the **Flexi Task** supports multiple paths so we do not need to put the **Flexi Task** into a **Set a Condition** action

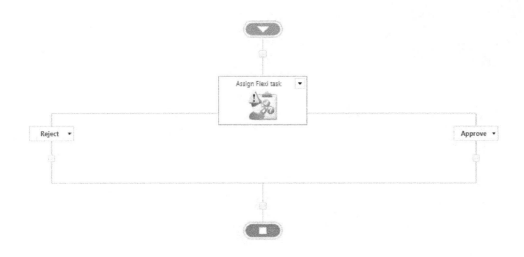

- Click the drop down arrow on the upper right of the **Flexi Task** action and click **Configure**

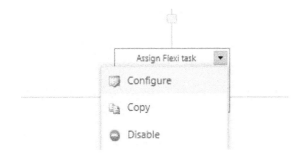

- On the **Configure Action** dialog click the address book icon to the right of the **Assignees** field

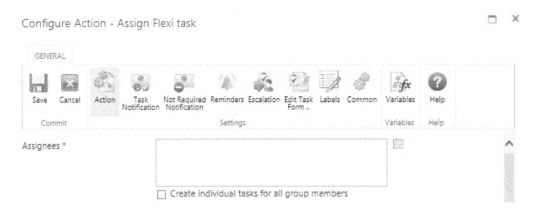

- On the **Select People and Groups** dialog click **Lookup** and then choose **Manager**

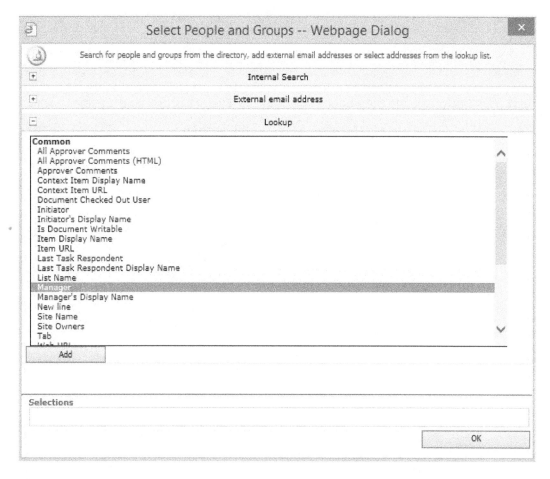

- Click **Add** and **OK**

- Select **Allow Delegation** and enter *A document requires your review* as the Task Description

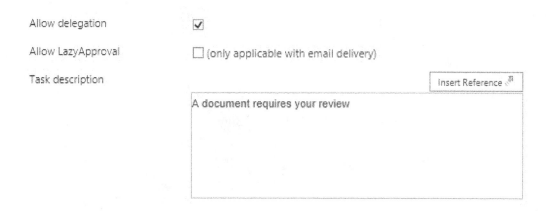

- Click **Task Notification** in the ribbon. Note that the **Flexi Task** will send an email notification. You can alter the message in the rich text box at the bottom just as we did with the **Send Notification** action in the last demonstration

- Here is an example of a Flexi Task email sent to an Assignee

Wed 2/4/2015 11:51 AM
SharePoint
Response required

To   Michael McManus
Retention Policy   Deleted Items (30 days)   Expires   3/6/2015
ℹ This item will expire in 25 days. To keep this item longer apply a different Retention Policy.
   You replied to this message on 2/4/2015 11:51 AM.

                                                              Workflow Notification
_____

A task has been assigned to you regarding this item:

Sample 2

Click here to respond to the task.
Click here to view the workflow status.

_____

- Click on Not Required Notification in the ribbon. Note that the Flexi Task will send out another notification if the Assignee no longer needs to deal with the assigned task. For example the task may be assigned to multiple assignees with rules such that only one assignee needs to respond. If someone else responds to a task in this situation Nintex will send other Assignees an email letting them know their response is no longer required

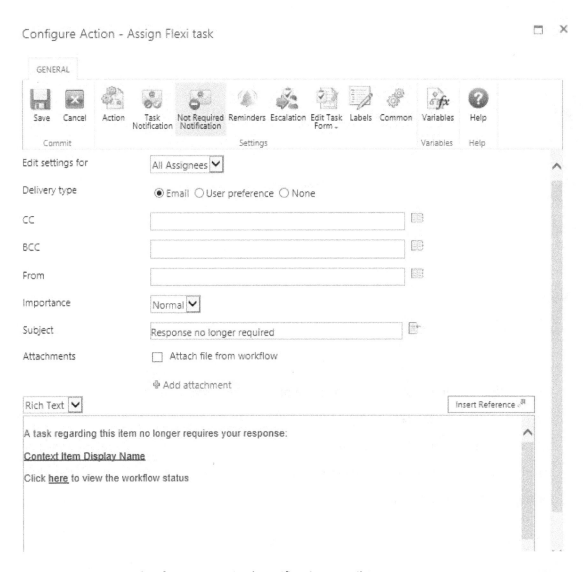

- Here is an example of a Not Required Notification email

Reply   Reply All   Forward

Wed 2/4/2015 10:45 AM

SharePoint

Response no longer required

To   Michael McManus

Workflow Notification

A task regarding this item no longer requires your response:

Sample 2

Click here to view the workflow status

- Click the **Reminders** icon on the ribbon. Note that you can set rules for reminders. A reminder is another notification Nintex will send out if someone does not complete their assigned task

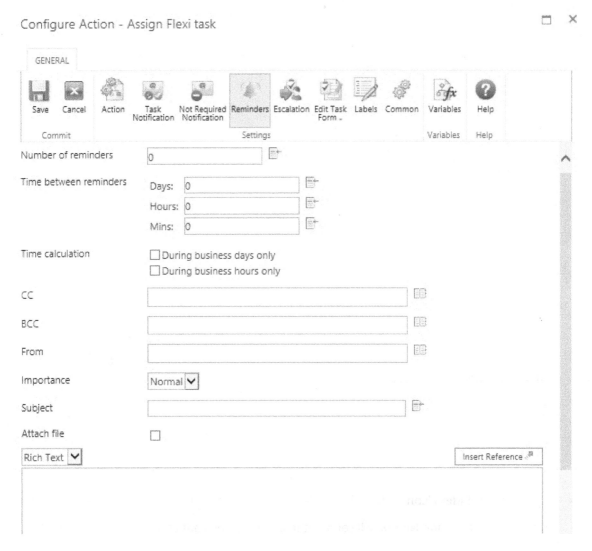

- The **Flexi Task** will handle the notification email so we do not need to use a Send Notification action.

- Similarly you can set escalation rules, to handle assigning the task to someone else entirely via delegation or pre-defined rules.

- The **Flexi Task** will not however update the **Approval Status** of the document being reviewed, so we do need to put some **Set Approval Status** actions in the workflow. The **Set Approval Status** action is in the **Lists and Libraries** section.

- Drag an **Set Approval Status** action into the **Flexi Task** under the **Reject** path

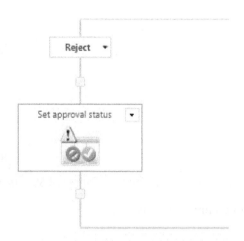

- Click **Configure** on the dropdown arrow on the upper right of the **Set Approval Status** action

- On the **Configure** page set the status to **Rejected** and **Save** the changes

- Drag an **Set Approval Status** action into the **Flexi Task** under the **Approve** path

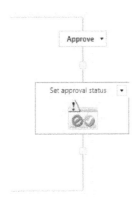

- Click **Configure** on the dropdown arrow on the upper right of the **Set Approval Status** action

- On the **Configure** page set the status to **Approved** and **Save** the changes

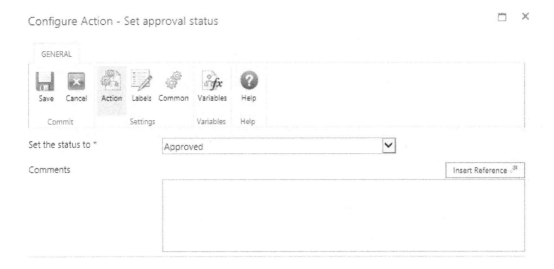

- **Save** and **Publish** the workflow

As the previous demonstration shows, we gain a lot of functionality when using a task to manage the approval as a process, rather than as a series of independent email notifications and list status updates.

Workflow Templates

Workflow Templates provide a shortcut. A template gives you a starting point, so that you do not have to repeatedly recreate workflows that reuse common actions. Nintex provides a number of templates.

Business Management / Finance

- Board Meeting Minutes Approval

- Disputed Invoice Process
- Business Performance Survey Review
- Travel Request
- Compliance Document Approval

Human Resources

- Absence Manager Approval
- Job Requisition
- Annual Leave
- Employee Benefits

Operations and IT

- Asset Tracking and Management
- Help Desk
- Create a New Employee
- Mail Enable Account
- Create an AD Security Group
- OCS-Enable an AD Account

Project Tracking / Product Management

- Project Budget Approval
- Project Issue Escalation

Sales / Marketing

- Lead Activity Process
- Marketing Plan Approval
- Simple Sales Process

Creating / Saving as a Workflow

You can also create your own Workflow Templates. After configuring a workflow the way you want it, simply save that workflow as a template:

Workflow Settings

Workflow Settings allow you as the workflow author to define general, workflow wide configuration settings such as:

Title and Description

Title and description

Title *	New Workflow
Description	A description of the workflow

Workflow Initiation

Workflows can be started or initiated in a number of different ways:

- Manually - choosing the 'Require Manage List Rights' checkbox means that only a user with Manage List Rights permissions can manually start the workflow
- Automatically upon creating a new list item (not available for site workflows)
- Automatically upon editing an existing list item (not available for site workflows)
- Automatically on a scheduled basis (only available for site workflows)
- Automatically started by another workflow

Start manually ✔

Require manage list rights ☐

Start when items are created No

Start when items are modified No

General Options

Selecting Publish without validation means Nintex will not check or validate the workflow or the configuration settings of the workflow's actions prior to publishing. Selecting this box can be helpful to speed things up while testing but is not recommended for a production workflow.

Publish without validation ☐

Enable workflow to start from the item menu ☐

Menu item label

Menu item image URL _layouts/15/NintexWorkflow/Images/StartWorkflowECB.png

Menu item position 0

Enable custom history messages ✔

Create Workflow Status Column

Selecting to Create a Workflow Status Column adds a column to the associated list or library. The new column's name is the workflow name and the column displays a hypler link to the workflow's status page.

Workflow History

Nintex Workflow for SharePoint 2013 provides several ways for us to monitor the progress or status of both running and completed workflows. In order for Nintex and SharePoint to keep track of a everything the workflow does a workflow history list is needed. Generally you can just leave the default workflow history list selected, but if you want to keep workflow history for different workflows in different workflow history lists you can create new Nintex workflow history lists and assign each workflow to the appropriate workflow history list.

History list   NintexWorkflowHistory ▼

Workflow Status

- Click on the status of the workflow - In Progress, Completed, etc.

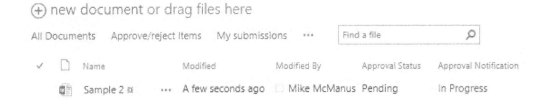

- The Workflow Status page will open showing basic information about the workflow

Workflow Information

Initiator: Mike McManus   **Document:** Sample 1
Started: 2/13/2015 9:57 AM   **Status:**   In Progress
Last run: 2/13/2015 9:57 AM

If an error occurs or if this workflow stops responding, you can end it.
□ End this workflow.

Tasks

This workflow created the following tasks. You can also view them in Workflow Tasks.

☐	Assigned To	Title	Due Date
	☐ Mike McManus	Workflow task	

Workflow History

The workflow recorded these events.

☐	Date Occurred	Event Type	User

There are no items to show in this view of the "NintexWorkflowHistory" list. To add a new item

- We can also see a visual depiction of the workflow which can be very helpful to track the progress on really long or complex workflows

- Using the ellipses for the document you uploaded click on **View Workflow History**

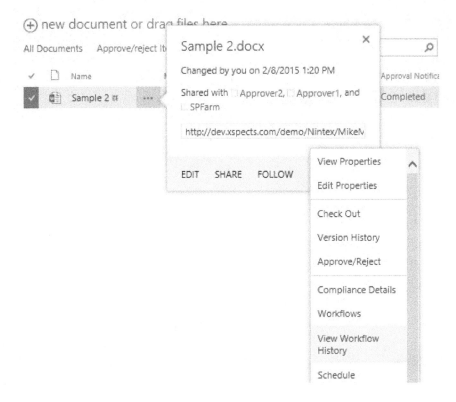

- Click the workflow instance you want to see

- This will open a visual depiction of the workflow. Note that both actions are green. This is because the workflow is complete, so we see a green path all the way from start to end. If the workflow was in progress, the actions that had not yet been completed would show as yellow

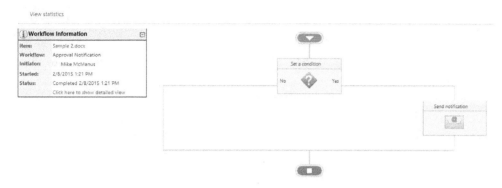

- If we click **_Click here to show detailed view_** it shows us:

The different options for seeing workflow history can be very helpful, especially when testing new workflows!

Task List

As discussed previously Nintex Workflows are Task driven, therefore you are required to select a workflow task list, whether you intend to create/assign tasks or not.

Form Type

Depending on what you have installed and the type of SharePoint license you have you will have options regarding how the Start form can be edited:

- Default
- Nintex Forms
- Custom

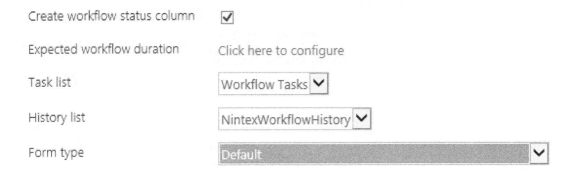

Association Columns

Association Columns are used to associate site columns with the workflow itself. Association columns are useful where you may need to reference columns from within a reusable workflow, or the workflow will not function properly. Association columns are automatically added to a list or library when a reusable workflow is associated to that list or library. For example if a particular status column is necessary using an Association Column ensures the column is present when the workflow runs.

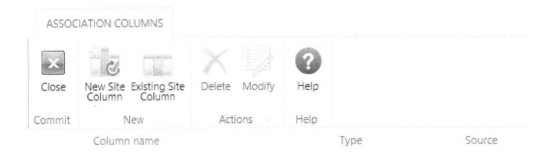

You will note that if necessary you can create a new SharePoint Site Column directly from within the Ninex Workflow interface.

Association Columns only work on list and library workflows (including reusable workflows).

Variables in Workflows

Workflows often need to save a value for future use. Workflow variables make creating and saving values very easy.

Workflow Variables

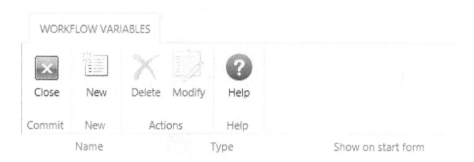

Workflow variables must be created before they can be used to store and retrieve values. New workflow variables must be defined by type:

- Single Line of Text
- Multiple Lines of Text
- Choice
- Number
- Date and Time
- Yes/No
- Person or Group
- Integer
- List Item ID
- Action ID
- Collection

Each new workflow variable can have a default value (or not, the default value is optional).

Create Workflow Variable ▢ ✕

WORKFLOW VARIABLES

💾	✕	❓
Save	Cancel	Help
Commit		Help

Name _____

Type

◉ Single line of text   ○ Person or Group
○ Multiple lines of text ○ Integer
○ Choice   ○ List Item ID
○ Number   ○ Action ID
○ Date and Time   ○ Collection
○ Yes/No

Default value _____

Show on start form   ☐

Each new workflow variable can also appear on the Workflow Start Form. The Workflow Start Form is seen when a workflow is started manually. Below is a screenshot of a Start form without any workflow variables visible.

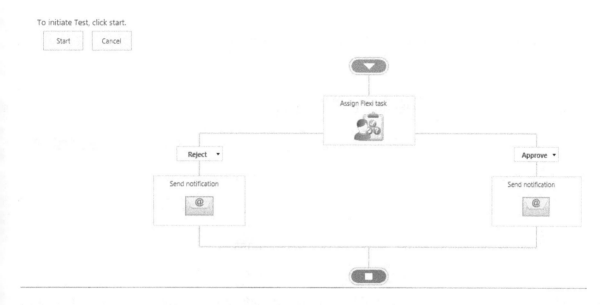

Remember that if you need a workflow variable to be seen and set on the Start form you probably do not want the workflow to start automatically.

Action Sets

An Action Set allows you to define reusable processes by grouping multiple Nintex Workflow Actions together. The Action Set can then be Copied or Saved as a User Snippet for re-use. Action Sets can also be run with elevated permissions allow you to design a workflow that creates or edits SharePoint items the individual user may not have permissions for.

Demo 3 - Using Action Sets and Variables

In this demo we will implement an Action Set

Action Sets are available in on-premises SharePoint

First add a new column to the library called WF Initiator's Email Address

- Click **Library Settings** on the **Library** tab of the ribbon

- On the **Library Settings** page we need to add some columns.

- Scroll down to the bottom of the **Columns** section and click **Create column**

- On the **Create Column** page enter *WF Initiator Email Address* as the **Column name**. Scroll down and click **OK**

Settings ▸ Create Column ⓘ

Name and Type	
Type a name for this column, and select the type of information you want to store in the column.	Column name:
	WF Initiator's Email Address

The type of information in this column is:

- ⦿ Single line of text
- ○ Multiple lines of text
- ○ Choice (menu to choose from)
- ○ Number (1, 1.0, 100)
- ○ Currency (£, ¥, €)

- Click the dropdown on the **Workflow Settings** icon on the Library tab of the ribbon and click **Manage Workflows in Nintex Workflow**

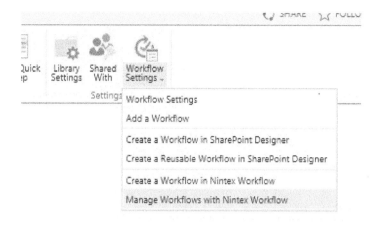

- Select the **Flexi Task Notification** workflow from the last exercise

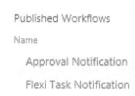

- Click **Workflow Settings** on the ribbon

- On the **Workflow Settings** page click **Variables**

Workflow Settings

- On the **Variables** page click **New**

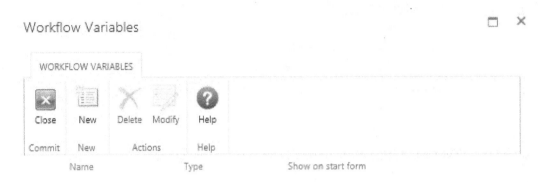

- On the **Create Workflow Variables** page enter *InitiatorsEmail* as the **Name** and click **Save**

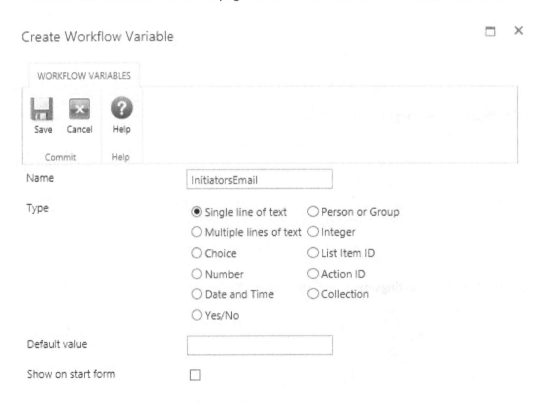

- Drag a **Query User Profile** action just below Start

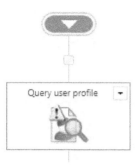

- Click the dropdown arrow in the upper right of the **Query User Profile** action and click **Configure**

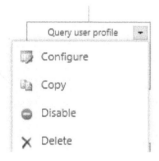

- On the **Configure Action** page click the address book icon to the right of the **User** field

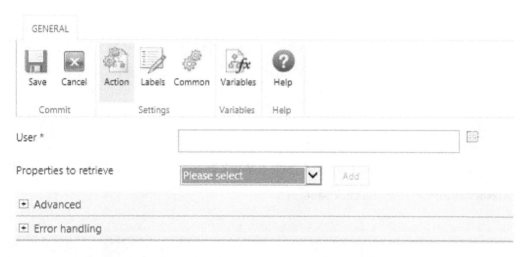

- Click the **Select People and Groups** page select **Lookup** and double click **Initiator** and click **OK**

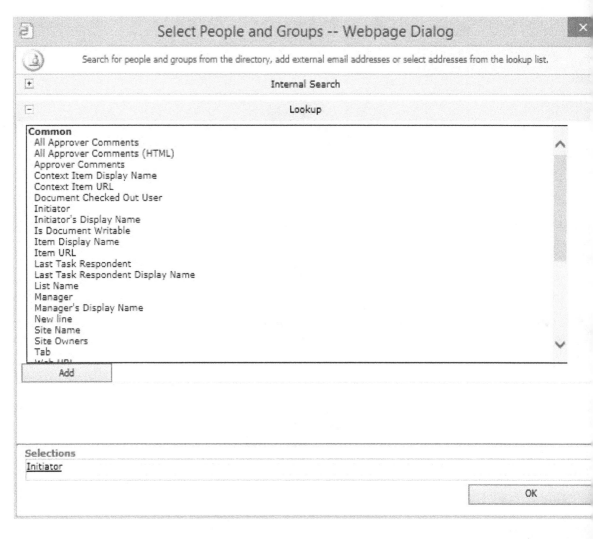

- In the **Properties to retrieve** dropdown select **Work Email** and click **Add.** Finally select the

  InitiatorsEmail variable and click **Save**

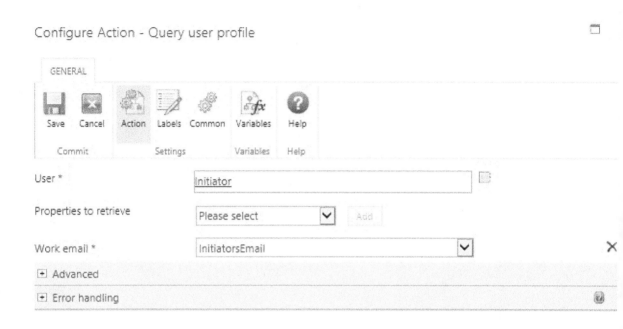

- Edit the **Flexi Task** to make yourself the **Assignee**

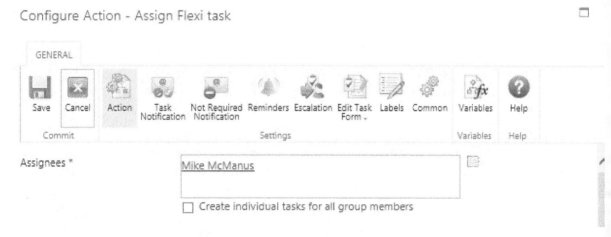

- Drag an **Action Set** (from the **Logic and Flow** section) action under the **Rejected Set Approval Status** action

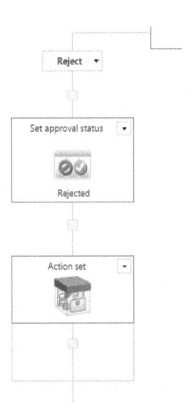

- Drag the **Rejected Set Approval Status** action into the **Action Set**

- Drag an **Update Item** action (the **Update Item** action is in the **Libraries and Lists** section) into the **Action Set** under the **Set Approval Status** action

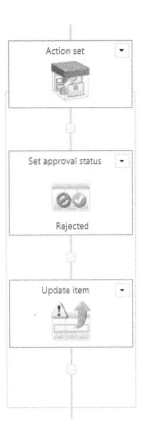

- Click **Configure** on the dropdown on the **Update Item** action's upper right corner

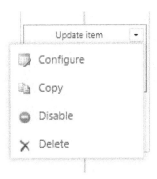

- On the **Configure Action** page select **Current Item** for the **Update** field. Select **WF Initiator's Email Address** as the **Field** to update. Finally set the **WF Initiator's Email Address** value to the **InitiatorsEmail** variable. Click **Save**

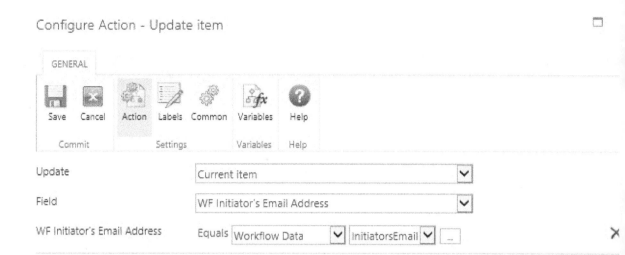

- Our Action Set should now look like

- Now we will save the **Action Set** so we can re-use it. Click the dropdown arrow on the upper right of the **Action Set** and click **Save as Snippet**

- **Name** the snippet and click **Submit**

- There is now a new section on the **Actions** panel called **My Snippets** which contains the snippet you just saved

- Now let's re-use the snippet in the **Approve** branch of the **Flexi Task**.

- First delete the **Set Approval Status** in the **Approve** branch

- Now that the **Approve** branch is empty drag your new snippet into the **Approve** branch

- You will notice that the **Action Set** looks like it is empty. Click the dropdown arrow in the upper right of your action set and click **Maximize**

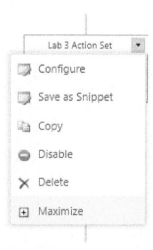

- Now you see the entire Action Set and all of the actions it contains

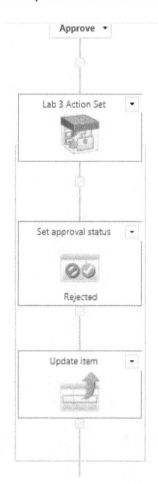

- We will need to alter the **Set Approval Status** action to set it to **Approve**

- Click the dropdown arrow in the upper right corner of the **Set Approval Status** action and click **Configure**

- Change the value to **Approved** and click **Save**

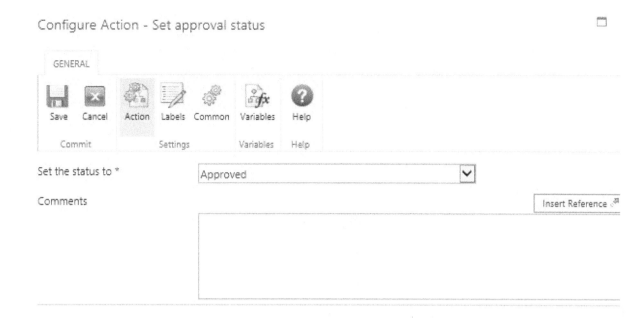

* **Save** and **Publish** the workflow

Workflow Actions

Workflow Actions are the building block of Nintex Workflows. Workflow Actions both define the workflow and execute desired automation functionality. Building a Nintex Workflow using Workflow Actions is basically a three

Workflow Action Configuration

If workflow actions are the building block of Nintex Workflows, the workflow action configuration page is the building block of workflow actions.

The Action Configuration page has a ribbon with different icons for different configuration settings for the workflow action selected. Each workflow action has different options for configuration. For example the image below is the workflow action configuration page for an Assign Flexi Task action:

Action

The Action settings on the Action Configuration page is where you set most of the action specific settings. For task type actions this page might include things like Assignees.

The example below is a screenshot of the Action settings for an Assign a Flexi Task action:

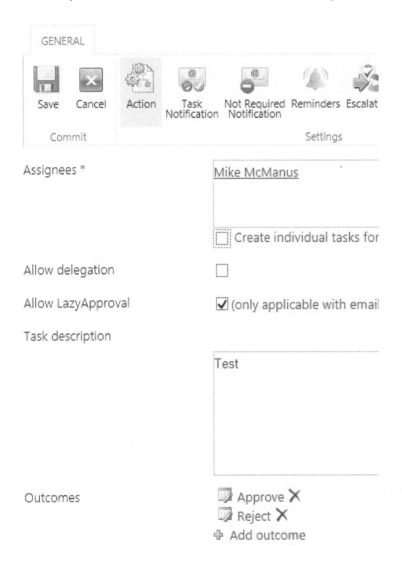

Labels

All workflow actions have labels. Each will have at least one default label indicating what kind of action it is. Best practices are to make the labels more specific, especially for complex workflows.

Each label can have:

- Top Label
- Bottom Label
- Right Label
- Left Label

For example here is an Assign Flexi Task action with the default label settings

And here it is with them modified

Note that the modified labels give a little more information about what the action does.

Common

The Common settings, while *Common*, are different for different workflow actions. The screenshot below is for the Assign a Flexi Task workflow action and is pretty representational of the Common settings.

- Expected duration - This allows you to indicate how long you thing this workflow should take. While not required this setting can be helpful to identify 'long running' workflow actions.
- Hide from workflow Status - This option allows you to opt the current action out of status reporting.
- Disable - The action will still exist but will not be executed. This can be very useful during de-bugging, or when you want to build out future functionality but not execute it.

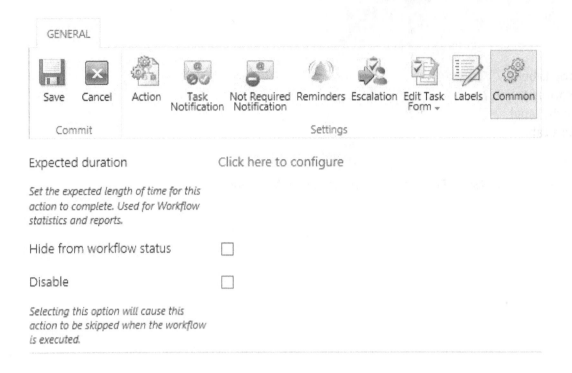

Insert Reference

The Insert Reference button/icon is a very useful tool in the Nintex Workflow Design interface. The Insert Reference button is presented in a number of different ways:

-
- ▤⁺

The Insert Reference interface provides you with commonly used dynamic values

Insert Reference

Common	Item Properties	Inline Functions	Workflow Variables

All Approver Comments
All Approver Comments (HTML)
Approver Comments
Context Item Display Name
Context Item URL

Note there are four tabs:

- Common - Provides commonly used values from within the workflow context
    - All Approver Comments
    - All Approver Comments (HTML)
    - Approver Comments
    - Content Item Display Name
    - Context Item URL
    - Current Date
    - Document Checked Out User
    - **Initiator**
    - **Initiator's Display Name**
    - Is Document Writeable
    - Item URL
    - Last Task Respondent
    - Last Task Respondent Display Name
    - List ID
    - List Name
    - **Manager**
    - **Manager's Display Name**
    - New line
    - Site Collection ID
    - Site ID
    - Site Name
    - Site Owners
    - Start Date
    - Start Time
    - Tab
    - Web URL
    - Workflow Instance ID
    - Workflow Log URL
    - Workflow Owner
    - Workflow Status URL
    - Workflow Title
- Item Properties
    -
- Inline Functions
- Workflow Variables

Browse

The Browse icon ⊞ is seen next to People and Group fields such as the Assignees field in an Assign Flexi Task workflow action

When you click the Browse icon you are presented with options for selecting users and groups from either Active Directory or SharePoint. You can also type in a specific email address.

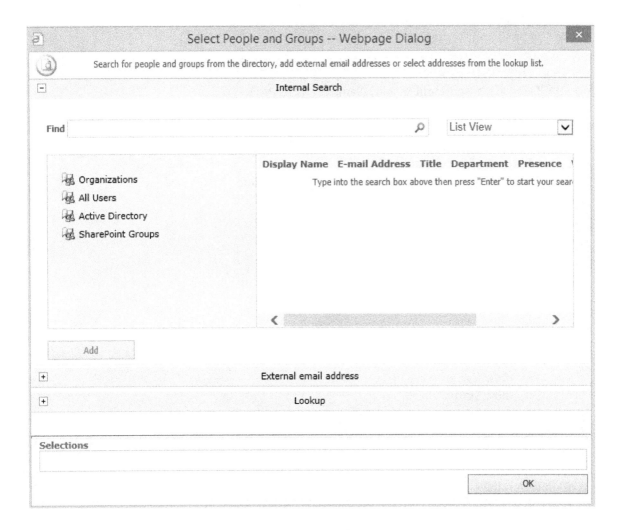

Notice that if you click Lookup you have the same options as the Insert Reference interface above

Common
All Approver Comments
All Approver Comments (HTML)
Approver Comments
Context Item Display Name
Context Item URL
Document Checked Out User
Initiator
Initiator's Display Name
Is Document Writable
Item Display Name
Item URL
Last Task Respondent
Last Task Respondent Display Na
List Name
Manager
Manager's Display Name
New line
Site Name
Site Owners

The ability to add these dynamic values really increases the flexibility and power of our workflows!

Workflow Action Groups

Workflow actions are grouped together on the left hand actions panel. The groups are based on similar functionality. For example the Integration Actions group contains workflow actions that for the most part extend functionality beyond SharePoint, into other systems; the Libraries and Lists group contains workflow actions that involve individual list items and library documents.

You can also search for a workflow action if you are not sure which group the action you are looking for is in.

Workflow Actions

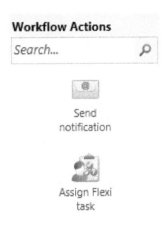

Send
notification

Assign Flexi
task

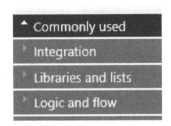

▲ Commonly used

▸ Integration

▸ Libraries and lists

▸ Logic and flow

Integration Actions

Integration Actions allow you to interact with external systems. In some cases getting information from external systems and in some cases (based on appropriate permissions) creating and modifying data in external systems.

- Call Web Service

The Call Web Service workflow action allows you to make a call to a SOAP web service and save returned values in a workflow variable

The Call Web Service workflow action requires a URL to the SOAP web service. Once the web service

has been discovered you must select a web method and provide credentials. The result can be stored in a workflow variable. In the screenshot below a web service call is being made to get a SharePoint list and the result is being saved in a Collection variable

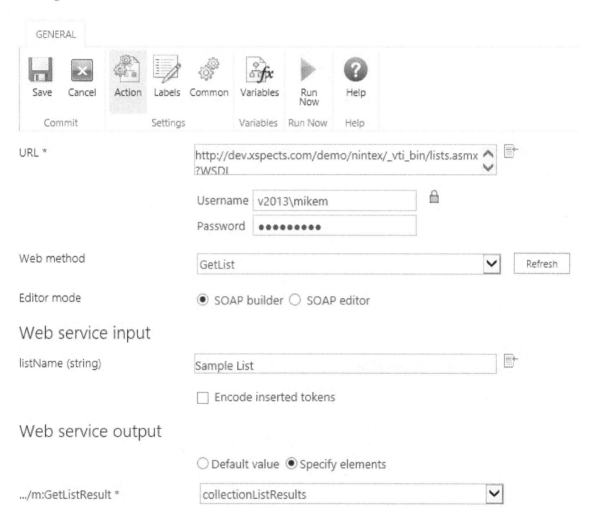

Note the **Run Now** button on the ribbon. Clicking Run Now will allow you to test the web service connection and verify that you are returning the results you expect.

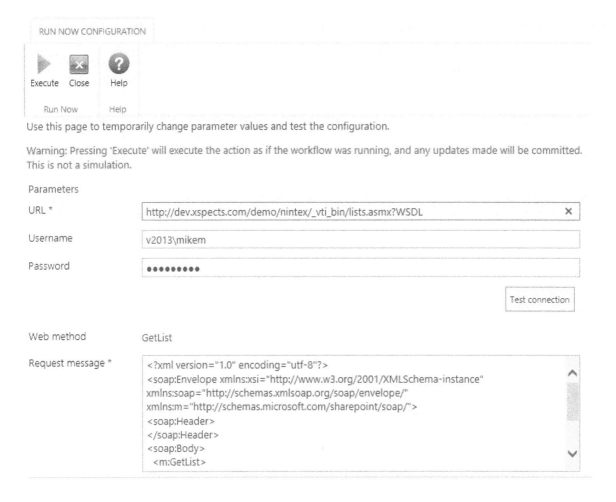

Clicking Execute results in the execution of the selected web method and displays the returned result

Results

```
<soap:Envelope xmlns:soap="http://schemas.xmlsoap.org/soap/envelope/"
xmlns:xsi="http://www.w3.org/2001/XMLSchema-instance" xmlns:xsd="http://www.w3.org/2001/XMLSchema">
  <soap:Body>
    <GetListResponse xmlns="http://schemas.microsoft.com/sharepoint/soap/">
      <GetListResult>
        <List DocTemplateUrl="" DefaultViewUrl="/demo/Nintex/Lists/Sample List/AllItems.aspx" MobileDefaultViewUrl=""
ID="{FB40A199-C66B-413C-B547-C22D7C5B15C8}" Title="Sample List" Description=""
ImageUrl="/_layouts/15/images/itgen.png?rev=23" Name="{FB40A199-C66B-413C-B547-C22D7C5B15C8}"
BaseType="0" FeatureId="00bfea71-de22-43b2-a848-c05709900100" ServerTemplate="100" Created="20150210
01:14:03" Modified="20150210 01:14:03" LastDeleted="20150210 01:14:03" Version="0" Direction="none"
```

- Create CRM Record

This workflow action allows you to create a new record in Microsoft CRM. You must provide credentials with sufficient permissions to create the CRM record.

Configure Action - Create CRM record

GENERAL

Save	Cancel	Action	Labels	Common	Variables	Help
Commit			Settings		Variables	Help

Dynamics CRM Version *   ● 4.0 ○ 2011 or later

Server URL *   http://[CRM Server URL]

Organization name *

Credentials *   Username
                            Password
                            Load CRM Details

Entity *

Store record ID in *

Attributes

- Delete/Disable CRM Record

Delete - Allows you to delete a record in Microsoft CRM. You must provide credentials with sufficient permissions to create the CRM record.

Disable - Allows you to disable a record in Microsoft CRM. You must provide credentials with sufficient permissions to create the CRM record.

Configure Action - Delete/Disable CRM record

GENERAL						
Save	Cancel	Action	Labels	Common	Variables	Help
Commit		Settings			Variables	Help

Dynamics CRM Version *	◉ 4.0 ○ 2011 or later
Server URL *	http://[CRM Server URL]
Organization name *	
Credentials *	Username _____ 🔒
	Password _____
	[Load CRM Details]
Action	◉ Delete ○ Disable
Entity *	⌄
Record to delete *	⌄

- **Execute SQL**

This workflow action allows you to execute a TSQL statement and save the returned results as a variable, usually a collection variable.

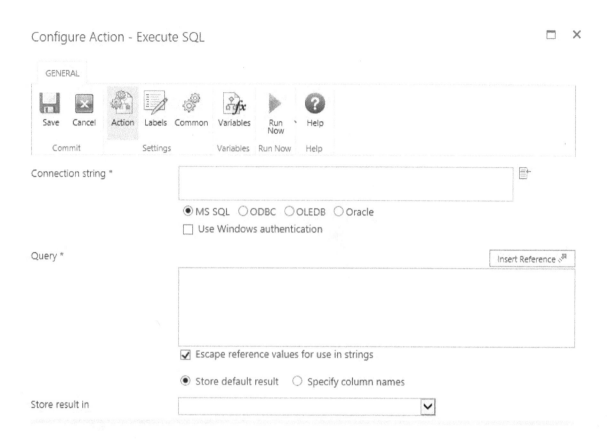

- Finder Users by Status

This workflow action will find and return user(s) with a specified OCS/Lync presence status. You can search for a single user, a SharePoint or Active Directory group. Multiple users and groups should be separated with a semi-colon.

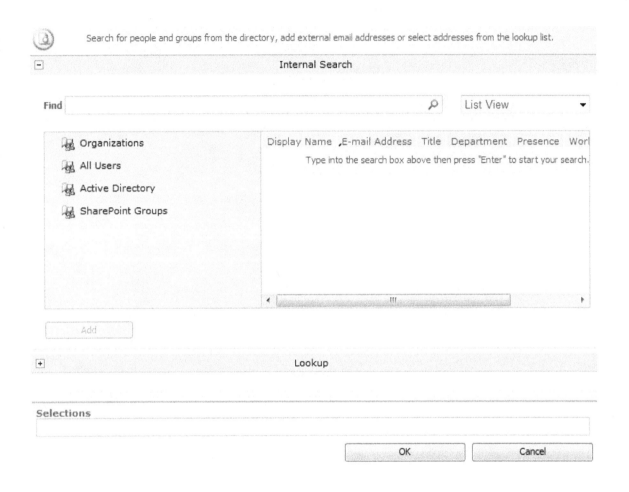

Returned results should be stored in a text or collection variable.

Note: Requires Office Communications Server 2007 or Lync Server 2010/2013 and the **Instant messaging settings** option in Global Settings must be set and configured

Instant messaging settings

The OCS/Lync settings to use when sending instant messages.

Changes to these settings will not take effect until there are no conversations in progress.

○ None   ● OCS/Lync

From sip address:

[   ]

From domain user (domain\username):

[   ]

Password:

[   ]

OCS/Lync server:

[   ]

Transport:

[TLS   ▼]

- **Get User Status**

This workflow action will return the OCS/Lync status of a selected user. Only a single user can be selected (no groups or multiple users).

The returned user should be stored in a variable.

Note: Requires Office Communications Server 2007 or Lync Server 2010/2013 and the **Instant messaging settings** option in Global Settings must be set and configured.

- Query BCS

The **Query BCS** action will retrieve data from the Business Connectivity Service (BCS). The BCS application must be created and configured prior to using the Query BCS action.

Configure Action - Query BCS

GENERAL

| Save | Cancel | Action | Labels | Common | Variables | Run Now | Help |

Commit   Settings   Variables   Run Now   Help

Credentials *

Username [   ] 🔒

Password [   ]

Application name * [⌄]

Instance name * [⌄]

Entity name * [   ]

➕ Add filter

Entity property to retrieve [   ] [Add]

Credentials

A valid username and password are required to access the BCS. This identity must have access to the external content type. If the external content type is configured to pass through credentials, the identity must also have access to the underlying data source.

Application name

The BCS application to query.

Instance name

The instance of the application to query.

Entity name

The type of entity in the BCS application to query.

Filter

BCS objects can be filtered to narrow the results returned

Click Add Filter and then enter the Filter Name and Filter Value

Filter name		✕
Filter value		

- Query CRM

This workflow action will retrieve data from Microsoft Dynamics CRM v4.0 and Microsoft Dynamics CRM 2011. The action mimics the Advanced Find functionality available in CRM.

Configure Action - Query CRM

GENERAL

Save	Cancel	Action	Labels	Common	Variables	Help
Commit			Settings		Variables	Help

Dynamics CRM Version * ● 4.0 ○ 2011 or later

Server URL * `http://[CRM Server URL]`

Organization name *

Credentials *

Username

Password

Load CRM Details

Attributes to return

Entity *

Return as ● XML ○ Variables

Store result in *

Filters

➕ Add filter

Dynamics CRM Version

Either version 4.0 or 2011 or later

Server URL

The URL of the CRM server

Organization name

The Organization located within CRM.

Credentials

The credentials used to connect to the CRM server and organization.

Attribute(s) To Return

The results returned can either be in XML or individual attributes can be specified and stored in a workflow variable.

Entity

The type of entity to be queried.

Return results as either a XML or as a variable (multiple return attributes require multiple variables)

XML: The returned results are structured as XML and all attributes of the primary entity will be returned for each record retrieved.

Variable: Each specified attribute will be returned and can be stored in a workflow variable.

Filter

BCS objects can be filtered to narrow the results returned

Click Add Filter and then enter the Filter Name and Filter Value

- Query Excel Services

This workflow action allows you to query data from an excel workbook and store the returned values.

Configure Action - Query Excel Services

GENERAL

Save	Cancel	Action	Labels	Common	Variables	Run Now	Help

Commit	Settings	Variables	Run Now	Help

URL   Web URL/_vti_bin/ExcelService.asmx

Credentials *   Username

                      Password

Workbook path *

Sheet name *

Update cell values

⊕ Add cell to update

Cells to retrieve *

Store result in *

Retrieve as formatted text   ☐

URL

URL to the excel services web service.

Providing this URL is optional. If the URL is left blank, this action will use the default excel services URL based on the URL of the site workflow is running on.

Credentials

Username and password

Valid credentials to access the Excel Services web service. The credentials must have access to the workbook.

Workbook path

The location of the Excel workbook to query. The workbook must be in a configured Excel Service trusted location.

Sheet name

The name of the Excel sheet in the workbook that will be queried.

Update cell values

Specifies cells that should be set in the workbook before data is retrieved. Changes to these cell values are not committed to the workbook, they are only used to determine the values of the cells to retrieve information.

Multiple cells can be updated by clicking the **Add cell to update** link.

Cell position the location of the cell to update. The cell location must be specified in the 'A1' format or be the defined name of a cell.

Cell value the value to update the cell with.

Cells to retrieve

The range of cells to retrieve values from. A single cell must be specified in the 'A1' format.

Store result in

The workflow variable to store the resulting value in.

If the selected variable can only contain a single value and a range is returned, only the first cell in the range will be used.

In a collection, values are stored left to right, top to bottom. For example, if the range to return is A1:B3, the values will be stored in this order: A1, A2, A3, B1, B2, B3.

- Query LDAP

The **Query LDAP** action allows the workflow to query a LDAP compliant data source such as Microsoft Active Directory. This action is for advanced users.

Configure Action - Query LDAP

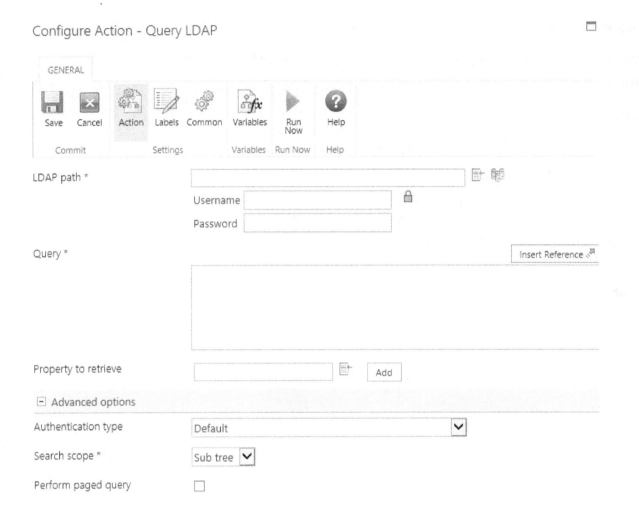

LDAP Path

To configure the **LDAP Path**, refer to the LDAP Picker for more information.

Query

Select the LDAP query to run. The query can be added manually or use the Inserting reference fields to include runtime values in the query.

Property to retrieve

The property to retrieve for the item found. More than one property may be retrieved.

Authentication type

Specify the method used to authenticate to the LDAP server.

Search scope

Determines how the query should behave. The default search scope is *Sub tree*.

Perform paged query

Check to specify that paging should be enabled on the result set.

- Query User Profile

This workflow action queries user profiles and returns user profile properties.

Configure Action - Query user profile

GENERATAL

Save	Cancel	Action	Labels	Common	Variables	Help
Commit			Settings		Variables	Help

User *

Properties to retrieve   Please select   Add

☐ Advanced

Credentials   Username

                   Password

User

The login name of the user whose profile should be queried. Multiple users can be specified.

Properties to retrieve

A list of available profile properties that the action can read. More than one property may be retrieved.

Credentials

The username and password of an account with access to profile attributes

Results returned should be stored in a collection variable.

- Query XML

This workflow action allows you to read and return XML data.

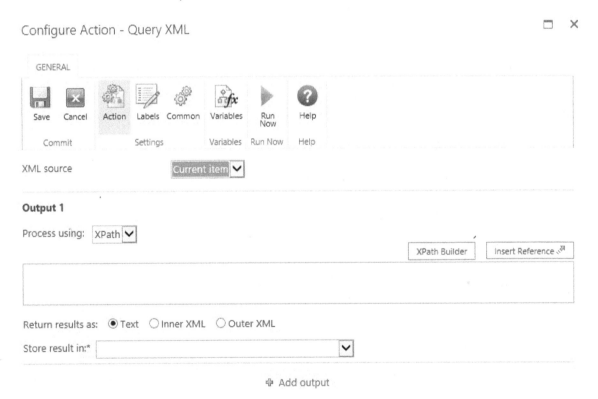

XML Source

The XML source can be selected from these three options:

Current item: The item in the list or library to which this workflow is associated.

URL: A URL to the XML source to be processed. A username and password can be specified when accessing the URL.

XML: Direct XML entered in the configuration dialog.

Process using

None: The resulting XML will not be processed. This allows the reading of the XML file or source without processing.

XPath: Allows querying of XML to retrieve data from a node or node set

XSLT: Allows the transformation of XML.

Return results as

Return query results as text, inner XML or outer XML.

Store result in

Use the drop-down to specify where the resulting text should be stored. More than one output value may be entered. To specify additional output select **Add output** and fill in the required information.

- Search Query

This workflow action allows you to query the SharePoint search index and return results

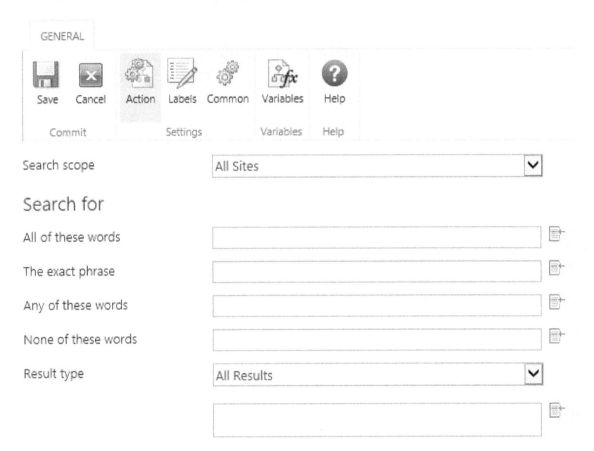

Property restrictions

Where the property

Select a property ▾

Equals ▾

[   ] 📑

➕ Add property restriction

Search results

Properties to return *

☐ AboutMe
☐ Account
☐ AccountName
☐ acronym
☐ acronymaggre

Results as XML ☐

Store result in * [▾]

Search scope

The search scope to use for the search

Search for

Search terms or keywords.

Result type

Specify a file type filter for the search.

Property restrictions

Allows further narrowing of the search results by only returning items where the property restriction rules are true.

Properties to return

Determines which property data will be retrieved from the search result. Multiple properties can be selected.

Results as XML

This option specifies whether to return the result set in an XML string. Returning the results as XML allows further processing and styling to be applied with the Query XML workflow action. A text workflow variable must be chosen to store the result if Return as XML is selected.

Store result in

Specifies the workflow variable to store the search results in. Unless a single result is expected a collection variable should be used.

- Send / Receive BizTalk

This workflow action allows you to send messages to BizTalk 2006 or receive messages from BizTalk 2006.

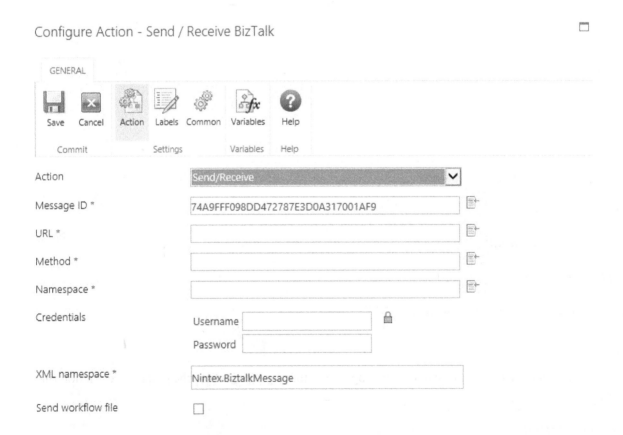

Data to send	Common	
	☐ All Approver Comments	⌃
	☐ All Approver Comments (HTML)	
	☐ Approver Comments	
	☐ Context Item Display Name	⌄

Export to XSD

Data to receive	*No workflow variables created.*

Export to XSD

Action

Send, Receive or Both

Message ID

A unique identifier that is used by Nintex Workflow when the BizTalk message handler receives a message.

URL

The URL of the published BizTalk web service.

Method

The web method of the web service to invoke.

Namespace

The namespace of the web service.

Credentials

Username and password, if required, to access the web service.

XML Namespace

The XML Namespace for the messages that are generated.

97

Send Workflow file

This option allows the current workflow item to be sent to BizTalk, instead of defining individual data from the workflow

Data to send

Allows selection of the data that must make up the message to send to BizTalk.

Data to receive

Allows selection of the data that is expected in a message from BizTalk. Only workflow variables can be selected.

Export to XSD

Nintex Workflow generates the schema file for both the 'data to send' and 'data to receive' messages.

- Update CRM Record
This workflow action allows you to update records in Microsoft CRM 4.0 and CRM 2011.

Configure Action - Update CRM record

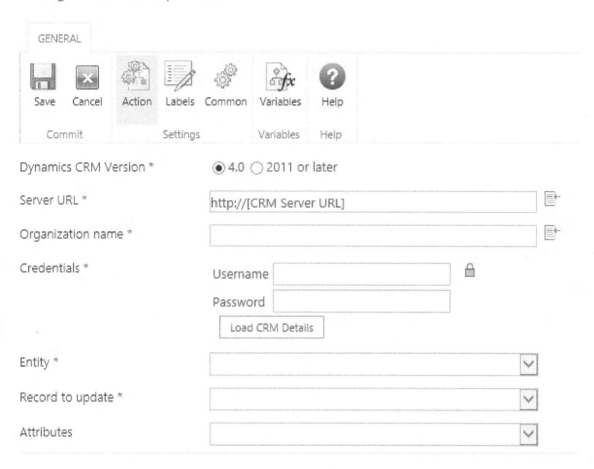

Dynamics CRM Version

The endpoint version of the Microsoft Dynamics CRM server to connect to.

Server URL

The URL of the CRM server to connect to.

Organization name

The Organization located within CRM.

Credentials

The credentials used to connect to the CRM server and organization.

Entity

The type of CRM record to be updated.

Record to update

Specify the GUID of the CRM record to be updated.

Attributes

Selecting an Entity will load any required and Business Required attributes.

- Update XML

This workflow action allows you to update XML data

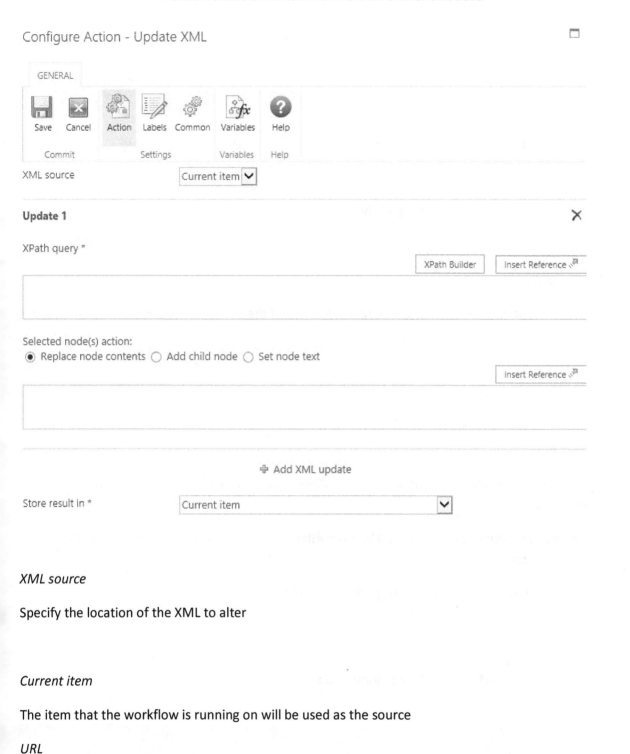

Configure Action - Update XML

XML source

Specify the location of the XML to alter

Current item

The item that the workflow is running on will be used as the source

URL

Data located at a nominated URL will be used as the source. A username and password can be provided for the request.

Updates

A number of update operations can be performed by a single Update XML action.

XPath query

The XPath query to the XML nodes that will be altered.

Selected node(s) action

The operation to perform on the selected node. Select one of the following options:

Add XML update

Select to define another update operation.

Store result in

Specifies where the resulting XML should be stored. Select Workflow variables type or choose from the following options:

Current item: The contents of the item will be overwritten with the new XML. Use this to update InfoPath form items.

URL: The XML will be stored at a location specified by a URL.

- Web Request

This workflow action performs an HTTP request to a URL.

Configure Action - Web request

GENERAL

Save	Cancel	Action	Labels	Common	Variables	Run Now	Help
Commit			Settings		Variables	Run Now	Help

URL *

Username

Password

○ GET ● POST ○ SOAP 1.1 ○ SOAP 1.2 ○ Other

Content type *   application/x-www-form-urlencoded

⊟ Add headers

⊕ Add header

● Text ○ Send workflow file

Insert Reference

Keep alive ☐

Allow auto redirect ☐

Store result in

Store http status in

Store response headers in

Store response cookies in

Url

The URL to which the HTTP request will be made

Credentials

The credentials that will be used for authentication to the URL. If no credentials are provided, the request will be made anonymously.

Operation

The Web Request action is capable of making many common HTTP calls.

Add headers

Specify the headers to be sent with the web request. Multiple headers can be selected by choosing the **Add header** option.

Text

Specifies the textual data that is sent as the body of the web request. This option is available for all operations except **GET**. To include a base64 encoded copy of the file that the workflow is running on in the request text, type in [FileData] and it will be replaced at run time (libraries only).

Send workflow file

Specifies that the bytes of the file on which the workflow is running should be sent as the web request body. This option is only available for workflows that are created on a document library.

Keep alive

Allows for the **Keep alive** option to be specified for the request.

Allow auto redirect

Allows for the **Auto redirect** option to be specified for the request.

Store result in

The workflow variable of text type in which to store the contents of the response.

Store http status in

The workflow variable text or number type in which to store the numeric http response code.

Store response headers in

The workflow variable of collection type in which to store each response header.

Libraries and Lists

The Libraries and Lists group of Nintex Workflow Actions provide functionality to create, modify and delete library and list items.

- Capture Document Set Version

This workflow action allows you to retrieve the current version of a document set.

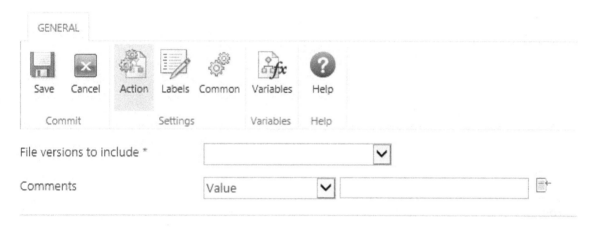

File versions to include

Latest major version only

Latest major or minor version

Comments

Add comments to the version retained

- Check In Item

This workflow action allows you to check in an item to a SharePoint library or list

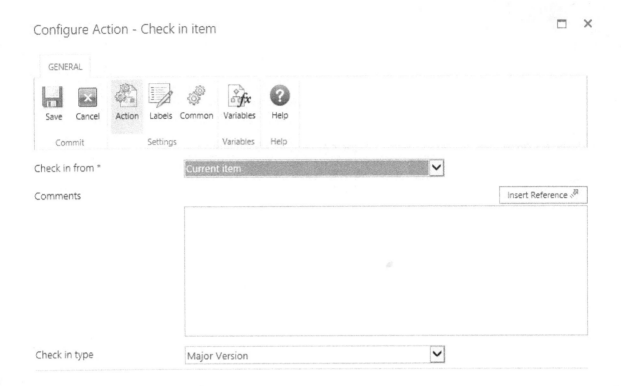

Check in from

Select the list or library to check the item into.

Comments

Add comments to the version retained

Check in type

Major Version

Minor Version

Overwrite - No Version Change

- Check Out Item

This workflow action allows you to check out an item from a SharePoint library or list

Configure Action - Check out item

Check out from * | Current item | ⌄ |

Check out from

Select the item to be checked out

- Convert Document

This workflow action allows you to convert a file from one format to another. This action can also be used to create a copy of an existing file (simply choose the same file format for the source and destination files).

This workflow action requires Word Automation Services are configured and running in SharePoint.

Configure Action - Convert document

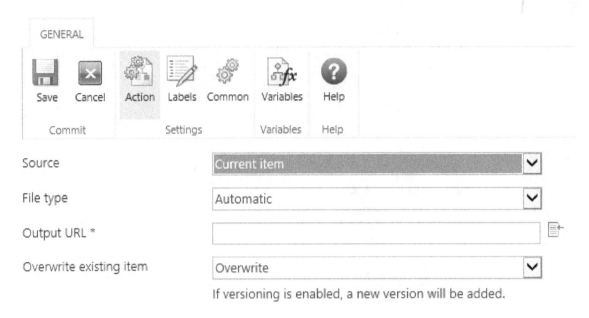

Source	Current item
File type	Automatic
Output URL *	
Overwrite existing item	Overwrite

If versioning is enabled, a new version will be added.

Source

The file to be converted/copied

File Type

The file type to be converted/copied to. Choose the same file type as the source file to perform a copy.

Output URL

Where should the converted/copied file be saved to

Overwrite

Overwrite

Create a new version

Do not overwrite (will fail if a file is already present)

- Copy Item

This workflow action allows you to copy an item from one SharePoint list to another. Files must be located in the root of the list or library (they may not be located in a folder).

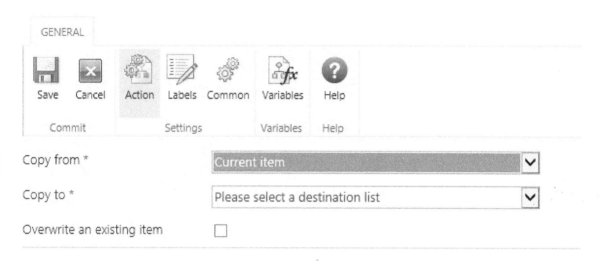

Copy from

The source item

Copy to

The destination list (where will the item be copied to). Only lists in the current site are available.

Overwrite

Yes/No

- Copy to File Share

This workflow action allows you to copy a SharePoint library item (file) to a local or network file share.

Configure Action - Copy to file share

GENERAL

Save Cancel Action Labels Common Variables Help

Commit | Settings | Variables | Help

Destination *

Example: \\server\share

Overwrite an existing item ☐

Username *

Password

Destination

The location to copy the file to. This must be a valid UNC path.

Overwrite

Yes/No

Credentials

Username and password

- Copy to SharePoint

This workflow action allows you to copy an item from the current list to another list or library within SharePoint. This action is very similar to the Copy Item action, except that it allows copying to another SharePoint site or site collection.

Configure Action - Copy to SharePoint

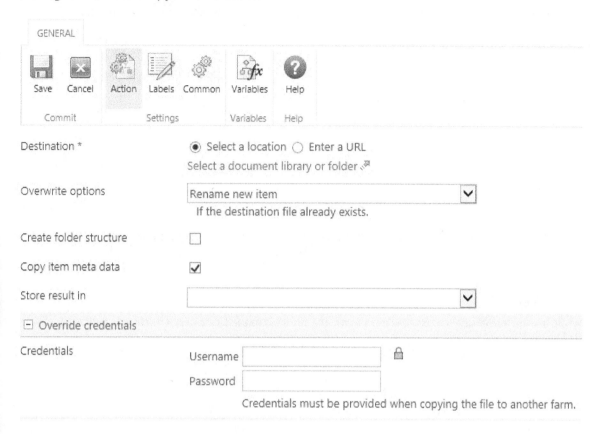

Destination

Select a location enables you to select a list or library in a visual tool

Enter a URL allows manual entry of the destination URL.

Overwrite options

Remove existing item

Rename new item

Update existing item

Create folder structure

Check this box to replicate a folder structure in the target library if the item being copied is in a sub folder. This option is not applicable when the destination is a remote SharePoint environment.

Copy item meta data

Check this box to set the item properties on the target item to the same values as the source item. Only matching fields will have their values copied.

Store result in

Stores the new URLs of the copied files into a text or collection variable.

Override credentials

Enter a Username and Password if the destination uses different permissions that the current site.

- Create Item

This workflow action allows you to create an item in a SharePoint list or library in the *current* site.

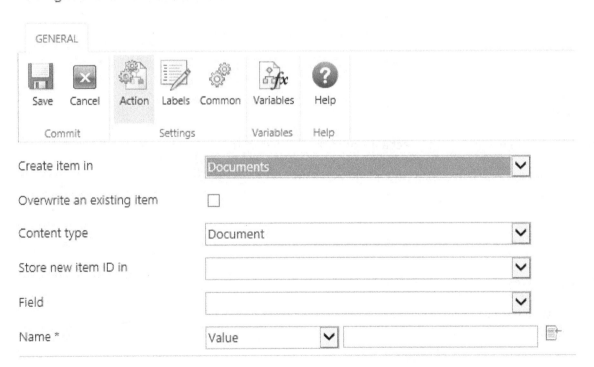

Create item in

Used to select a destination list - where will the new item be created?

Content Type

Defines what type of item will be created. If a document type is selected the default file template will be used.

Overwrite an existing item

To overwrite an existing item in the destination library tick this check box. If this option is not selected, an identifier will be appended to the filename. This applies to libraries only.

Store new item ID in

The created item will be assigned an ID. This new item ID can be stored in a List Item ID Workflow Variable.

Field

Available fields that can be added to the created item will be dependent on the content type in the destination list.

- Create Item in Another Site

This workflow action allows you to create an item in a SharePoint list or library in the *another* site

Configure Action - Create item in another site

Item location

Site *	⦿ Select site ○ Enter a URL
	Nintex Demo ⬀
List *	Please select ▾
Folder	

Item details

Content type	▾
Field	▾
Store new item ID in	▾

Site

The target site for the new item (destination).

Select site: Select a site via a visual interface

Enter a URL: Manually enter a URL to the site.

List

Drop down list containing available **Lists** at the target location

Folder

Select a folder or enter a folder name

Content Type

Select a content type for the destination item. The selected content type must be available in the target list.

Field

Available fields that can be added to the created item will be dependent on the content type of the target list.

Store new item ID in

The created item will be assigned an ID which should be stored in a List Item ID Workflow Variable.

- Create List

This workflow action allows you to create a list in the current web application.

Configure Action - Create list

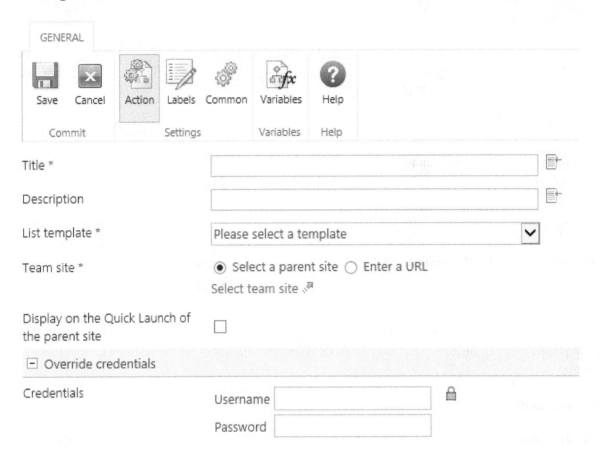

Title

The Title is the name of the new list.

Description

The Description is a brief statement about the new list.

List template

The SharePoint list template that will be used to create the new list.

Team site

The Team site is the site or sub-site in which the new list will be created.

Display on the Quick Launch of the parent site

Allows you to add a link to the new list on the Quick Launch left navigation of the parent SharePoint site.

Override credentials

Allows you to provide credentials to use when creating the new list. This can be useful when the users initiating the workflow do not have sufficient permissions on the target list.

- Declare as Record

This workflow action allows you to declare an item as a Record. Record restrictions are dependent upon Record Declaration settings.

The Declare as Record workflow action does not have any configuration options, other than labels.

- Delete Drafts

This workflow action allows you to delete the draft (or minor versions) of the current item.

The Delete Drafts workflow action does not have any configuration options, other than labels.

- Delete Item

This workflow action deletes an item in a list within the current site.

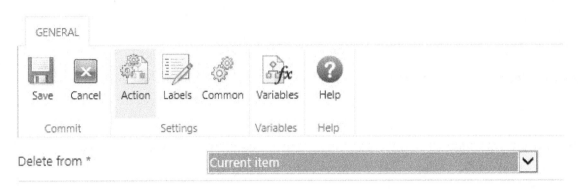

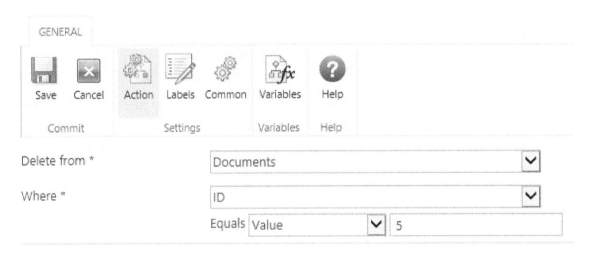

Delete from

Select the list and list item to delete

- Delete Multiple Items

This workflow action allows you to delete multiple items from a list within the selected site.

Configure Action - Delete multiple items

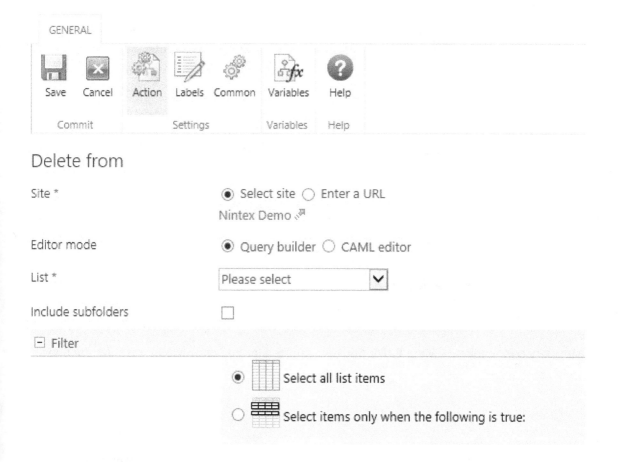

Site

The target site where items are to be deleted.

Select site: Enables a site picker (Select a team site) to navigate through the portal structure and select the target location.

Enter a URL: Allows manual entry of the URL or selection using Inserting reference fields.

Editor Mode

CAML editor: Use the CAML Editor mode to create more advanced cross list queries. View the CAML at any time by switching to the CAML Editor mode.

Query builder: Build queries for a single list for the site specified using a visual interface

List

Drop down list containing available Lists at the selected site.

Include subfolders

Yes/No

Filter

You can filter the query to further restrict deleted items

CAML Query

The CAML query editor appears when **CAML Editor** is selected in the **Editor Mode**. Displays the CAML query being constructed.

- Delete Previous Versions
Use this workflow action to delete all previous versions (minor and major) of the current item

The Delete Previous Versions workflow action does not have any configuration options, other than labels.

- Discard Check Out
Use this workflow action to discard the 'check-out' of an item within the current site.

Configure Action - Discard check out

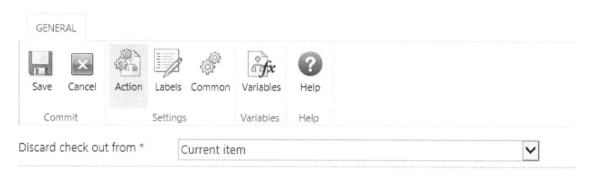

Configure Action - Discard check out

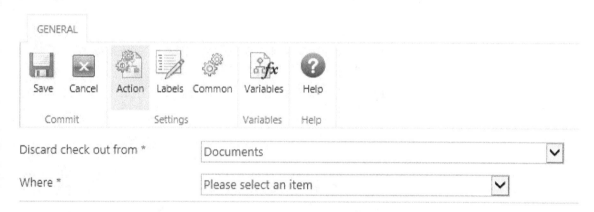

Discard check out from

Select either the Current item that the workflow is running on, or one of the available libraries.

Where

If not selecting the Current item you can specify a filter to select specific items

- Query List

This workflow action allows you to query a list within the current site and return the list items as a Collection workflow variable.

Configure Action - Query list

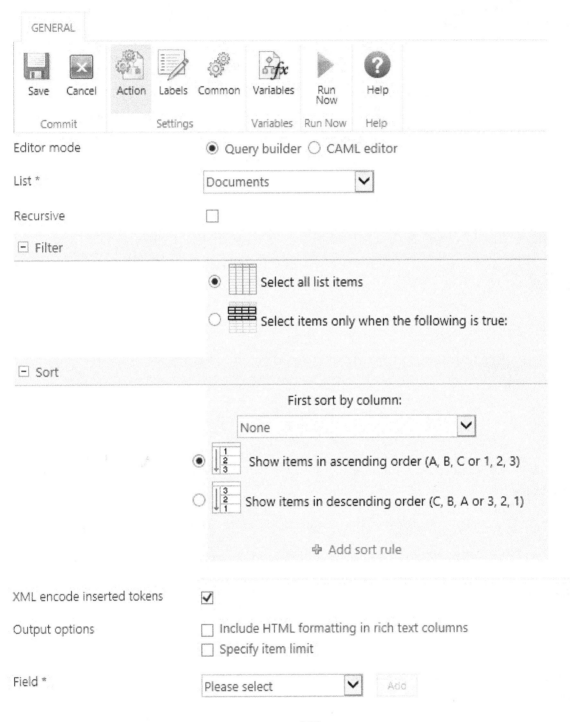

Editor Mode

Choose whether to use the UI to build the query, or edit the CAML manually.

CAML editor use the CAML Editor mode to create more advanced cross list queries. View the CAML at any time by switching to the CAML Editor mode.

Query builder can build queries for a single list in the same team site as the workflow.

Editor Mode: Query Builder

In Query builder mode, the following elements will build the query:

List

Select the list to query data from. Lists in the current team site are displayed.

Recursive

Check this option to query for items within folders and subfolders.

Filter

The criteria that nominated list items must match in order to be selected.

Sort

The order in which selected values should be returned.

XML encode inserted tokens

This option ensures that the inserted tokens will be encoded and is able to support special characters.

Output options

Include HTML formatting in rich text columns

Specify item limit

Field

The field to retrieve the data from. More than one field can be selected.

Editor Mode: CAML Editor

When CAML editor is selected, the query can be run on either the current site or an alternate site to the one the workflow is running in.

To query an alternative site, select the Alternative site option and enter the Site URL to a SharePoint site. The site must exist in the same farm as the workflow, but can be in a different site collection or web application.

When the Alternative site is selected, the Query builder mode is disabled.

- Read Document

This workflow action allows you to read the placeholder (content controls) values from within a Microsoft Word document. This workflow action is dependent upon Microsoft Word Automations Services running and configured in the SharePoint farm.

The word document being read must be in the .docx format.

Configure Action - Read document

GENERAL						
Save	Cancel	Action	Labels	Common	Variables	Help
Commit			Settings		Variables	Help

Source	Current item
Content control title *	
Store in *	

Source

The document where the 'content control' is to be read from.

Content control title

The title of the 'content control' within the document.

Store in

Select the Workflow variable to store the value retrieved from the 'content control' within the document. If more than one value is being returned select a Collections workflow variable.

- Send Document Set to Repository

This workflow actions allows you to send a Document Set to a Record Repository or a Record Center. The Content Organizer feature must be enabled on the site to route documents by properties.

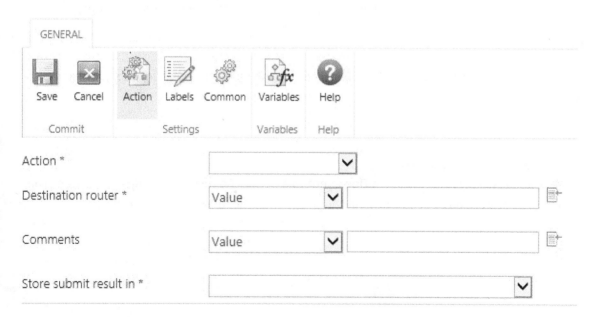

Action

Copy

Move

Move and Leave a link

Destination Router

Enter the URL to the Content Organizer for the destination site.

The URL can be found in the Submission Points section of the 'Content Organizer: Settings' page of the destination repository, and usually contains /OfficialFile.asmx'.

Comments

The information to be added to the audit log when the document set is sent to the repository.

Store submit results in

This refers to the 'submit result' provided by SharePoint on the status of the submission, for example: 'Success'.

- Send Document to Repository

This workflow actions allows you to send a Document to a Record Repository or a Record Center. The Content Organizer feature must be enabled on the site to route documents by properties.

Configure Action - Send document to repository

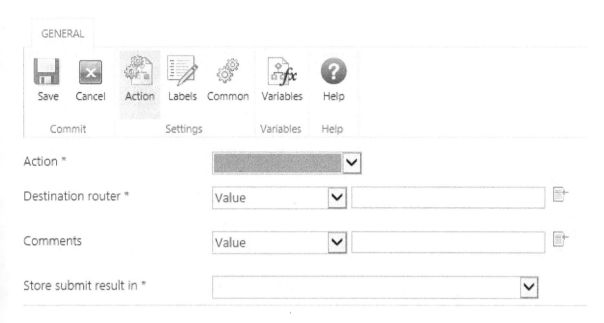

Action

Copy

Move

Move and Leave a link

Destination Router

Enter the URL to the Content Organizer for the destination site.

The URL can be found in the Submission Points section of the 'Content Organizer: Settings' page of the destination repository, and usually contains /OfficialFile.asmx'.

Comments

The information to be added to the audit log when the document is sent to the repository.

Store submit results in

This refers to the 'submit result' provided by SharePoint on the status of the submission, for example: 'Success'.

- Set Approval Status

This workflow action allows you to set the Approval Status for the current item. Content Approval must be enabled on the list.

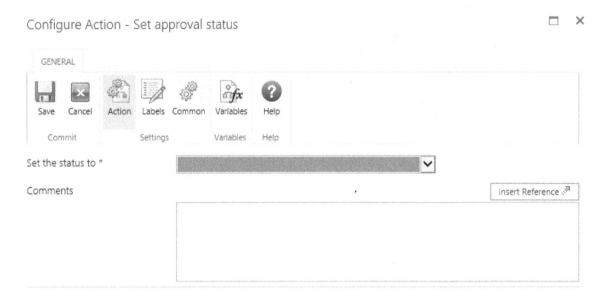

Set the Status to

Approved

Rejected

Pending

Draft

Scheduled

Comments

The comments entered here will be associated with the update to the status of the item

- Set Document Set Approval Status

This workflow action allows you to set the Approval Status for the current Document Set. Content Approval must be enabled on the library.

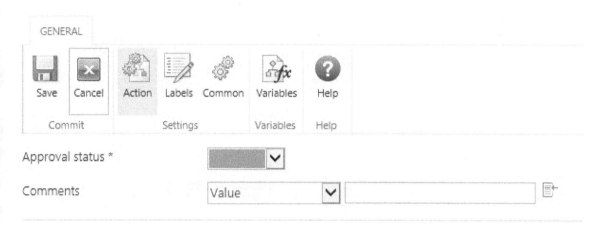

Set the Status to

Approved

Rejected

Pending

Comments

The comments entered here will be associated with the update to the status of the item

- Set Field Value

This workflow action allows you to set the value of a field (column) within the current item.

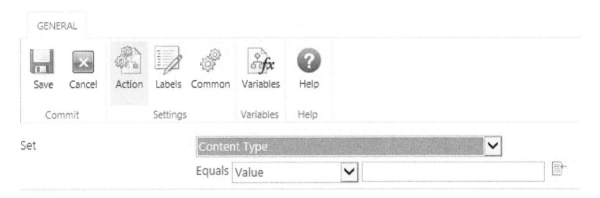

- Set Item Permissions

This workflow action allows you to modify permissions for a single item. This can be very useful when item level permissions are needed.

Configure Action - Set item permissions

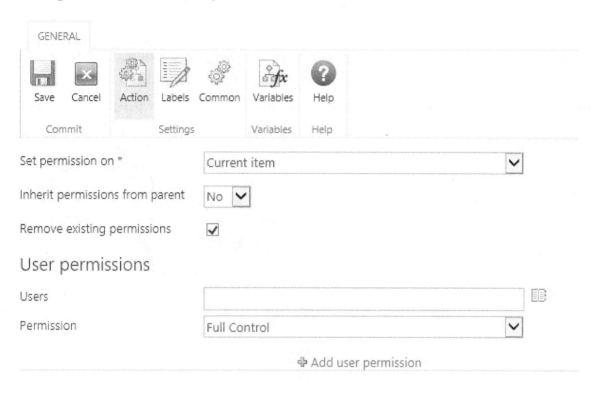

Set permission on

Select the item to set permissions for

Inherit permissions from parent

Yes

No

Remove Existing Permissions

Yes

No

User(s)

Select a user or group to assign access permissions for the item.

Permission

The level of permission that can be assigned to a user or group for the item.

- Update Document

Use this workflow action to update placeholders or content controls within a Microsoft Word document. This workflow action is dependent upon Microsoft Word Automations Services running and configured in the SharePoint farm.

The document must be in the .docx format

Configure Action - Update document

GENERAL

Save	Cancel	Action	Labels	Common	Variables	Help

Commit | Settings | Variables | Help

Source — Current item

□ Add content control values

Content control title

Value

Preserve formatting ☐

⊕ Add content control value

Output — Current item

Source

The document where the 'content control' is to be read from.

Content control title

The title of the 'content control' within the document.

Value

The value to update the content placeholder to

Preserve Formatting

Yes

No

Output

Current Item

Output URL

- Update Item

This workflow action allows you to update the values of multiple fields (columns) for an item within the current site

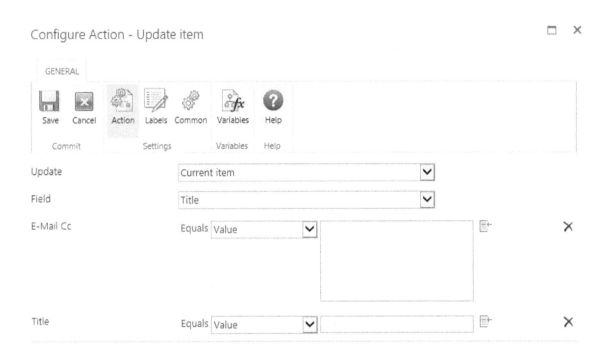

Update

Select the item to update from a list within the current site

Field

Select the field(s) to update

- Update Multiple Items

This workflow action allows you to update the values of multiple fields (columns) for multiple items in a selected site

Configure Action - Update multiple items

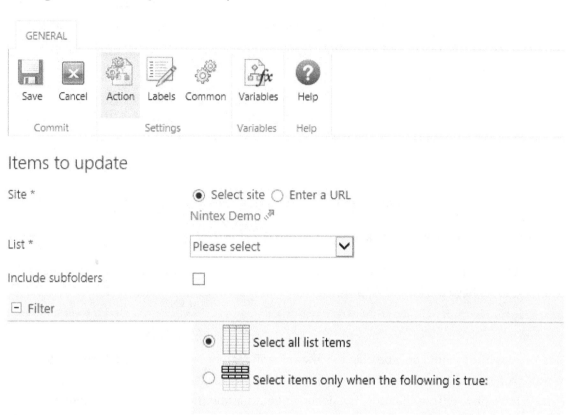

Items to update

Site *   ⦿ Select site ◯ Enter a URL
                    Nintex Demo

List *   [Please select ▾]

Include subfolders ☐

⊟ Filter

⦿ |||| Select all list items

◯ ▦ Select items only when the following is true:

Fields to update

Field   [None ▾]

Site

Select a site or enter a URL

List

Select the item to update from a list within the selected site

Field

Select the field(s) to update

Demo 4 - Create List Items with Item Level Unique Permissions

SharePoint is generally a pretty easy system to manage permissions for because permissions are generally managed at either the site or list/library level. When things get tricky is when we want to do things like give very specific permissions for each individual item in a SharePoint list, such as each document in a library.

Take this Use Case as an example:

We have a SharePoint document library that we store proposals in.

We want all of Sales Team to be able to add proposals to the library.

We want the author's Manager to be the assigned Approver for submitted proposals; which means that each document could have a different Approver.

Each Sales Team Author should only be able to view and edit his/her own submitted documents. A Sales Team Author should not be able to even view the submitted proposals of other Sales Team Authors. This means that we have ensure that only the document author and the author's Manager have permissions to even view the document.

Each Manager should only be able to view and approve the proposals submitted by authors they manage.

The Document library used in this Demo is named 'Proposal Library'.

All employees who will be submitting proposals are in the 'Sales Team' SharePoint group.

The 'Sales Team' SharePoint group has 'Contribute' permissions on the 'Proposal Library'. This is so all the 'Sales Team' members can add to the library. No other permissions have been granted for the library.

We will create a workflow that upon document creation sets the unique item level permissions based upon the parameters above.

- Navigate to the **Proposal Library**

- On the **Library** tab of the ribbon and click **Create a Workflow in Nintex Workflow** under the **Workflow Settings** dropdown

- When the Workflow Designer opens click **Settings** on the ribbon. On the **Workflow Settings** page enter **Set Unique Permissions** as the **Title** and select **Yes** to **Start when items are created**

Workflow Settings

WORKFLOW SETTINGS

Save   Cancel   Variables Association Edit Start Manage Start Variable   Help
                           Columns   Form -   Order

Commit   Settings   Help

Title and description

Title *   Set Unique Permissions

Description

Workflow options

Start manually   ☑

Require manage list rights   ☐

Start when items are created   Yes ▾

Start when items are modified   No ▾

Publish without validation   ☐

- **Save** the **Workflow Settings**

- Drag the Set Item Permissions action onto the design canvas

- Click the down arrow and click **Configure**

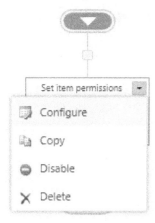

- On the **Configure** dialog select **No** for **Inherit permissions from parent** (this will ensure that only the permissions we assign here are valid, all others are removed)
- Ensure the box is checked for **Remove existing permissions**
- Under **User Permissions** click the **Browse** button

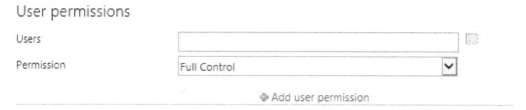

- On the **Select People and Groups** dialog select **Initiator** in the **Lookup** section

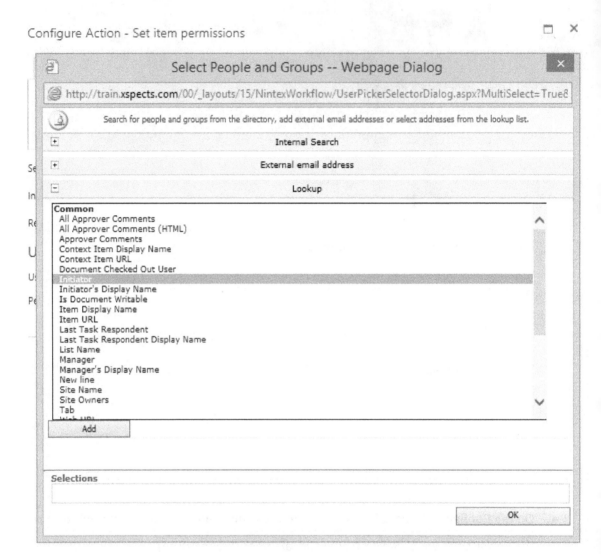

- Click **Add** and **OK**

- Select the **Contribute** permission level for the Initiator

- Click Add user permission

User permissions

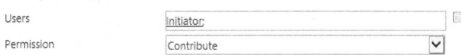

Users	Initiator;
Permission	Contribute

- Click the **Browse** button next to the new Users box

User permissions

Users	Initiator;	
Permission	Contribute ▾	
Users		
Permission	Full Control ▾	

➕ Add user permission

- On the **Select People and Groups** dialog select the **Manager** SharePoint Group in the **Lookup** section

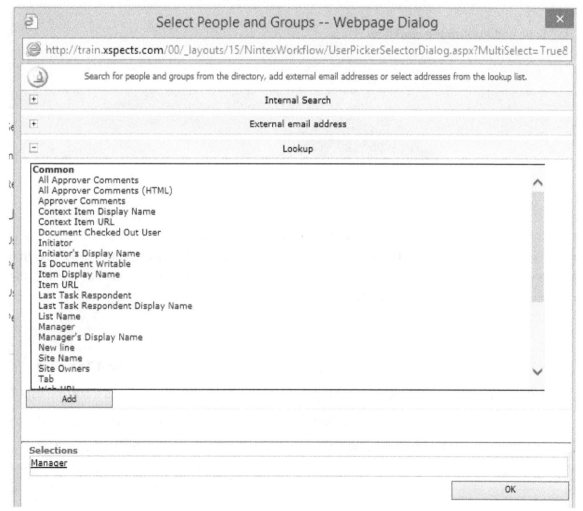

- Click **Add** and **OK**

- Select the **Approve** permissions level for the Manager

User permissions

Users	Initiator;
Permission	Contribute ⌄
Users	Manager
Permission	Approve ⌄

⊕ Add user permission

- **Save** and **Publish** the workflow

Demo 5 - Creating and Updating Documents

SharePoint uses a service called the Word Automation Service to create and modify Office Documents. Nintex Workflow contains actions that work in conjunction with the Word Automation Services. In this demo we will create a new document from a template, and then update the contents of the document using content controls inside the Word Document.

- We have already uploaded the Template file to a library called **Lab Document Template**
- First we need to create a new document library to store the certificates, and a custom list. The custom list will contain a column for an Employee's Name and a column for an award Month. These values will be used to update the controls inside the *Employee Award Template*

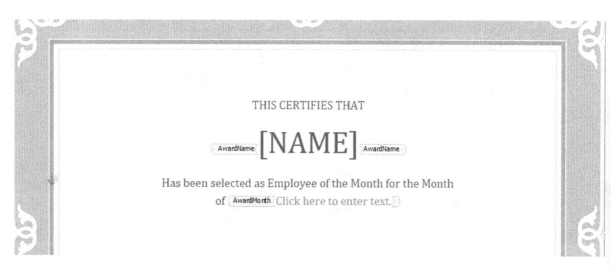

- On the **Gear** icon in the upper right click **Add an App**

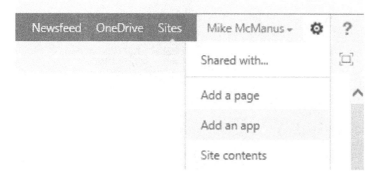

- On the **Your Apps** page click **Document Library** to create a new SharePoint list based on the **Document Library** template

Site Contents · Your Apps

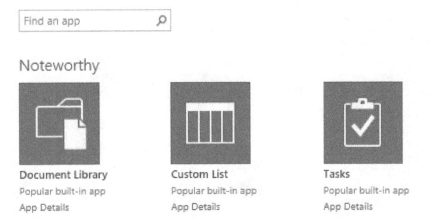

Find an app

Noteworthy

Document Library
Popular built-in app
App Details

Custom List
Popular built-in app
App Details

Tasks
Popular built-in app
App Details

- Name the **Document Library YourName_Award_Certificates**

Adding Document Library   ×

Pick a name
You can add this app multiple times to your site. Give it a
unique name.

Name:
MikeM_Award_Certificates

Advanced Options   Create   Cancel

- On the **Gear** icon in the upper right click **Add an App**

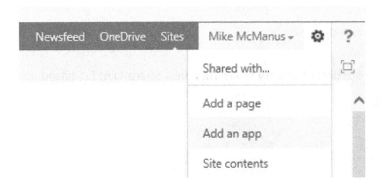

Newsfeed   OneDrive   Sites   Mike McManus ▾   ⚙   ?

Shared with...   ⊡

Add a page   ∧

Add an app

Site contents

- On the **Your Apps** page click **Custom List** to create a new SharePoint list based on the **Custom List** template

Site Contents · Your Apps

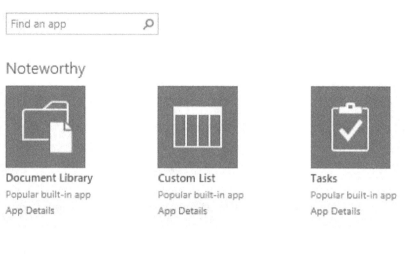

- Name the Custom List **YourName_Awards**

- Click on the new Custom List to open it
  - On the **List** tab of the ribbon click **Create Column** and create a column named **Awardee Name** of type Single Line of Text

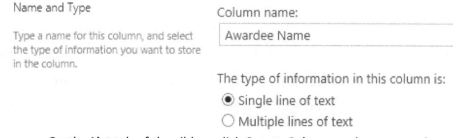

  - On the **List** tab of the ribbon click **Create Column** and create a column named **Awardee Month** of type Single Line of Text

Name and Type

Type a name for this column, and select
the type of information you want to store
in the column.

Column name:

Awardee Month

The type of information in this column is:

◉ Single line of text

○ Multiple lines of text

○ Choice (menu to choose from)

- On the **List** tab of the ribbon and click **Create a Workflow with Nintex Workflow** under the

  Workflow Settings dropdown

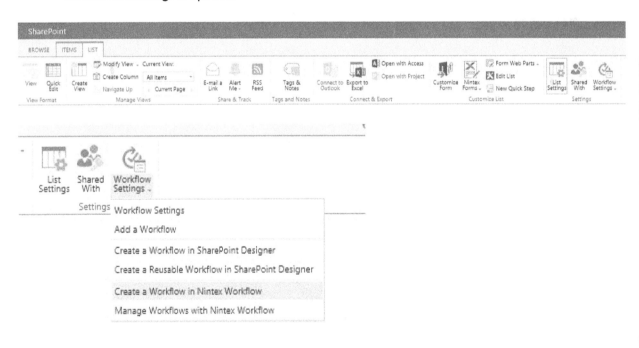

- When the Workflow Designer opens click **Settings** on the ribbon. On the **Workflow Settings**

  page enter **Employee Award** as the **Title** and select **Yes** to **Start when items are created**

Workflow Settings

WORKFLOW SETTINGS

Save	Cancel	Variables	Association Columns	Manage Start Variable Order	Edit Start Form	Help
Commit				Settings		Help

Title and description

Title *   Employee Award

Description

Workflow options

Start manually   ☑

Require manage list rights   ☐

Start when items are created   Yes

Start when items are modified   No

- Click **Workflow Variables**
- On the Workflow Variables dialog box create two variables of type single line of text:
    - Awardee Name
    - Awardee Month

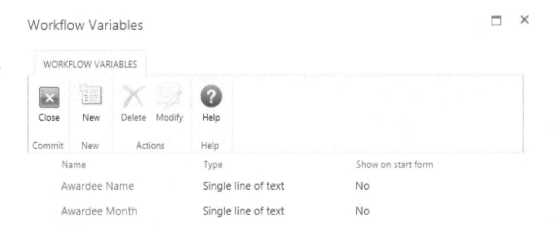

Name	Type	Show on start form
Awardee Name	Single line of text	No
Awardee Month	Single line of text	No

- **Close** the **Workflow Variables** dialog

- **Save** the **Workflow Settings**

- Drag the **Set Variable** action on the designer

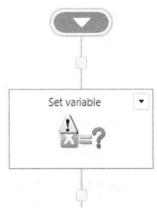

- On the **Configure** dialog enter the values as below and click **Save**

Configure Action - Set variable

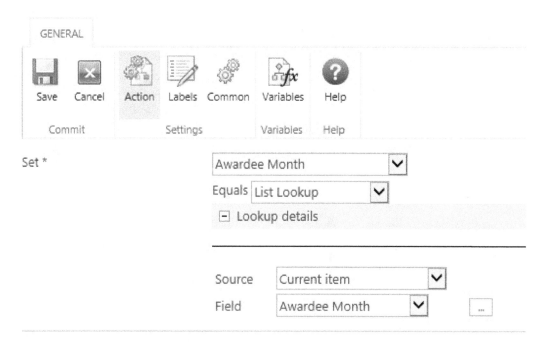

Set * Awardee Month

Equals List Lookup

⊟ Lookup details

Source Current item

Field Awardee Month

- Drag another **Set Variable** action on the designer

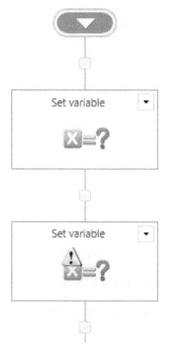

- On the **Configure** dialog enter the values as below and click **Save**

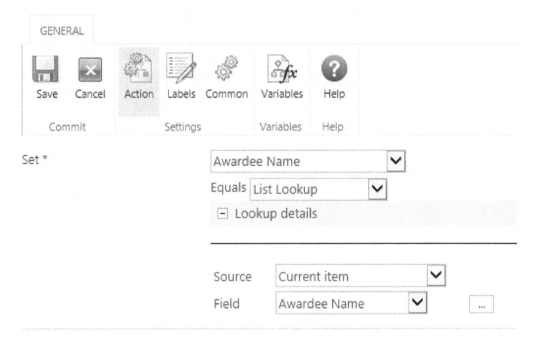

- Drag the **Convert Document** action onto the designer

- Click the down arrow and click **Configure**
- On the **Configure** dialog enter the values as below and click **Save**
- The **Source URL** value is the url to the **Lab Document Template/Certificate.docx**

- The **Output URL** value is the url to the your awards library plus a file name such as:

  MikeM_Award_Certificates/MikeM.docx

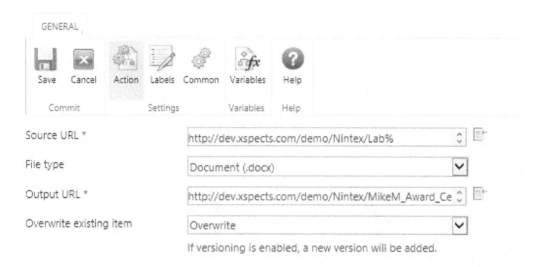

- Drag a **Commit Pending Changes** control under the **Convert Document** control

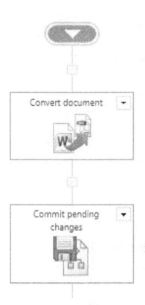

- The **Commit Pending Changes** action does not require any configuration

- Drag an **Update Document action** under the **Commit Pending Changes** action

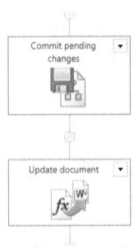

- Click the down arrow and click **Configure**

- On the **Configure** dialog enter the values as below

- **The Source URL** value is the url to the your awards library plus a file name such as: **MikeM_Award_Certificates/MikeM.docx** (it must be the same value you entered above in the **Convert Document** action for the **Output URL**)

- **The Output URL** value is the url to the your awards library plus a file name such as: **MikeM_Award_Certificates/MikeM.docx** (it must be the same value you entered above in the **Convert Document** action for the **Output URL**)

- Select **Overwrite existing item**

- **Content Control Title**

The content control title is the name of the placeholder inside the word document. In this demonstration the word document is the certificate.docx template file

THIS CERTIFIES THAT

Has been selected as Employee of the Month for the Month

of (AwardMonth (Click here to enter text.))

As you can see the template file has two content placeholders (AwardName and AwardMonth). We want to set the values of these two content placeholders with the values entered into our SharePoint list. It is very important that the content control title exactly matches what is in the word document.

So in this demonstration we need two content control title objects, one named AwardName and one named AwardMonth. We want to set the values of these content placeholders to the variables we set earlier.

- Enter the values as below and save the action. Remember to use the lookup to select the

    workflow variables:

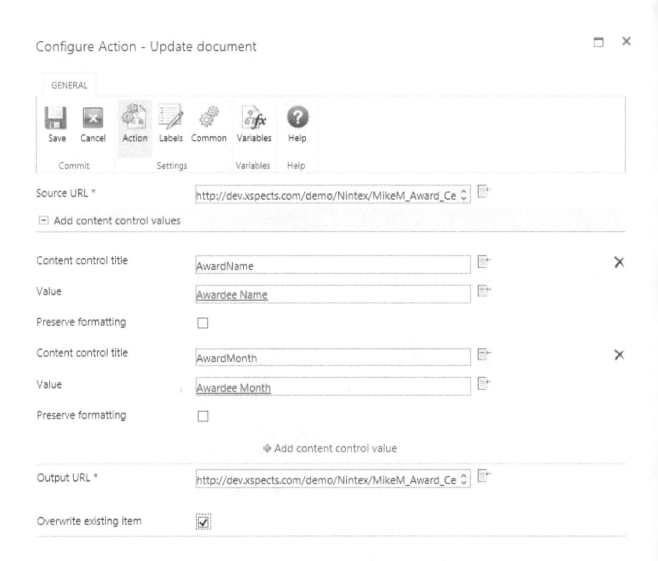

- Drag a **Commit Pending Changes** control under the **Update Document** control

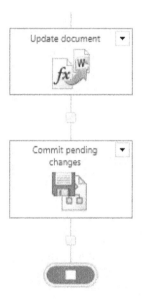

- The **Commit Pending Changes** action does not require any configuration
- **Save** and **Publish** the Workflow

Logic and Flow

The Logic and Flow workflow actions provide much of the functionality we will use to control how actions are processed, the order and sequence.

- Action Set

The Action Set workflow action allows you to group workflow actions together into a single re-usable unit.

Other workflow actions on the design canvas are dragged into the action set.

Under the Common Tab the Action Set can be set to execute under the permissions of the Workflow Author rather than under the permissions of the workflow initiator.

Configure Action - Action set

GENERAL

Save	Cancel	Labels	Common	Variables	Help
Commit		Settings		Variables	Help

Message to log on completion

Expected duration   Click here to configure

Set the expected length of time for this action to complete. Used for Workflow statistics and reports.

Hide from workflow status   ☐

Disable   ☐

Selecting this option will cause this action to be skipped when the workflow is executed.

Run as workflow owner   ☐

Checking this option will cause this action, and any child actions, to run using the credentials of the user who published the workflow instead of the user who started the workflow.

When an Action Set is configured to Run as workflow owner all actions within the Action Set will execute using the credentials of the user who created and published the workflow.

- State Machine

The State Machine workflow action is a container. The State Machine contains other workflow actions. Within the State Machine workflow actions can be repeated and re-routed, to accommodate use cases such as re-submitting items for approval after being initially rejected.

The State Machine can have multiple execution branches or States. Using the Change State workflow action State Machines re-direct execution to different execution branches. A State Machine usually has at least 2 states, but can have more.

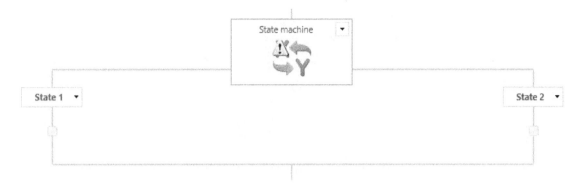

Configure Action - State machine

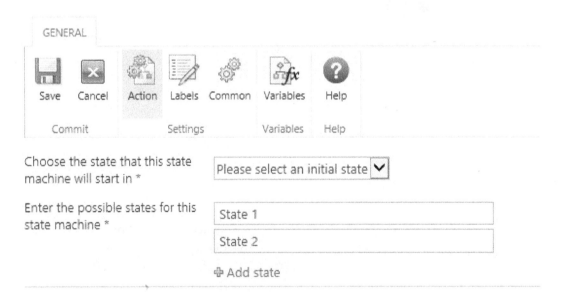

Initial State

An initial state must be selected. The initial state is the execution branch the state starts in

Possible States

You can modify or add multiple states (or execution branches) for the State Machine

- Change State

This workflow action must be used in conjunction with a State Machine workflow action. The Change State is used to change the current State of a State Machine workflow action (this re-directs the execution flow to the execution branch represented by the selected State).

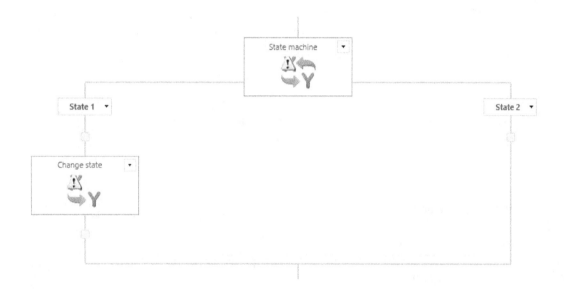

Configure Action - Change state

Next State

Select the State to switch to. Create all of the States/Execution Branches first.

- Commit Pending Changes

* FROM THE NINTEXWORKFLOW2013HELPFILE.PDF *

This workflow action forces all existing batched operations to be committed. Batched operations are operations performed by workflow actions that do not commit immediately.

For example, the "Update list item" action doesn't actually update an item immediately, it waits until the workflow commits. The workflow commits at a delay action, a task action or the end of the workflow. So when the update list item action runs, it just registers that it needs to update the item, the item actually updates on commit.

The SharePoint workflow engine doesn't necessarily commit batched operations in the order they are displayed on the designer.

For example, if the following actions are in this order:

Set item permissions action (Nintex)

Update list item action (Microsoft SharePoint)

Set permissions action (Nintex)

These would actually execute in this order:

Set item permissions action (Nintex)

Set item permissions action (Nintex)

Update list item action (Microsoft SharePoint)

It executes it in this order, because there are actually two batches, the Microsoft batch and the Nintex batch (any other third party has their own batch). This is because third parties cannot add operations to the Microsoft batch.

In addition, all items in a single batch are executed before actions in another batch. The batch that is executed first depends on the first activity: If the Microsoft SharePoint action was encountered first, then all the Microsoft actions would run before the Nintex actions.

The "Commit pending changes" action is another point where a workflow will execute all its batch operations.

So, modifying the above example:

Set item permissions action (Nintex)

Update list item action (Microsoft SharePoint)

Commit pending changes

Set item permissions action (Nintex)

In this case everything will run in order. The Nintex batch will run first because the Nintex action is first encountered, but in this scenario there is only one action in this batch. The "Update item" action will run. Then the workflow will commit, and the final "Set item permissions" action is in a new batch.

Use the Commit Pending Changes workflow action to ensure actions are executed in the order you intend. My general rule is if in doubt I use Commit Pending Changes.

- Filter

This workflow action ends the workflow if a configured condition is *not* met.

Configure Action - Filter

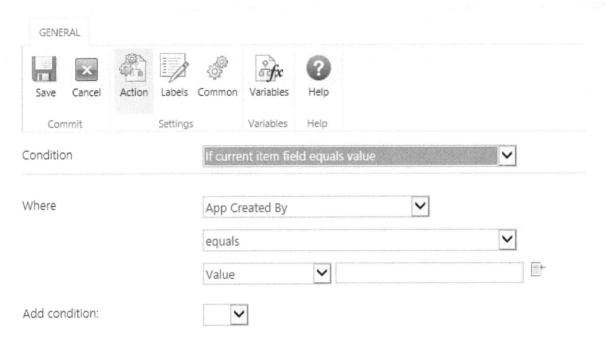

Condition

- If current item field equals value

This condition type evaluates if an individual field of the current item matches or compares to a certain value/column.

- If any value equals value

This condition allows the use of two fields, two workflow variables or two lookups to compare at runtime.

- Title field contains keywords

This condition allows a comparison to be performed that determines if the item's title contains certain specific words.

- Modified in a specific date span

This condition evaluates to true if the current item is modified between two specified dates.

- Modified by a specific person

This condition evaluates to true if the item has been modified by a specific person. The username is case sensitive.

- Person is a valid SharePoint user

This condition checks if the specified user is a member of the SharePoint site.

- Created in a specific date span

This condition checks if the item was created between the specified dates.

- Created by a specific person

This condition checks if an item was created by a specific user.

- The file type is a specific type

This condition checks if the file type extension of the current item is of the specified type.

- The file size is in a specific range kilobytes

This condition checks if the file size of a document is between the specified sizes, in kilobytes.

- Check list item permissions

This condition checks if the permissions of a specified user matches or is higher than the specified permission level provided for an item in a list

- Check list item permission levels

This condition checks if permission levels of a specified user matches or is higher than the permission levels for an item within this list.

These different methods for comparing values are also used in the Run If, Loop and the Set a Condition workflow actions.

- For Each

This workflow action is used to iterate or 'loop' through each item in a collection workflow variable. The 'For Each' workflow variable is also a container; other workflow actions are dragged into the For Each workflow action. Each action within the For Each workflow action will be repeated for each iteration of the loop.

Configure Action - For each

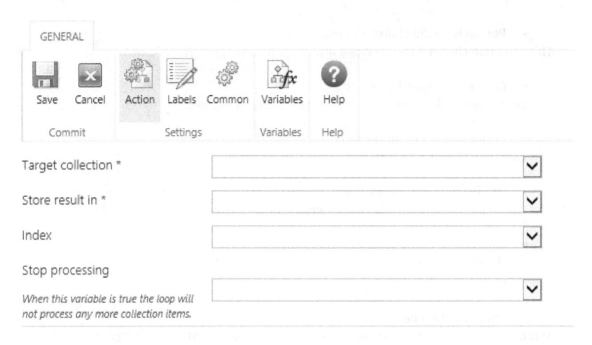

Target Collection

The collection variable to loop through.

Store result in

The current value in the Target Collection. This value changes with each iteration or 'loop' through the Target Collection.

Index

A workflow variable of type number, used to keep track of the position of the current item within the collection. The initial value is 0.

Stop processing

Yes/No

- Loop

This workflow action allows you to execute a group of workflow actions through multiple iterations, similar to the 'For Each' workflow action. The 'Loop' workflow action iterates or 'Loops' through items while a set condition remains true. Configuring a Loop workflow action is very similar to configuring a Set a Condition workflow action.

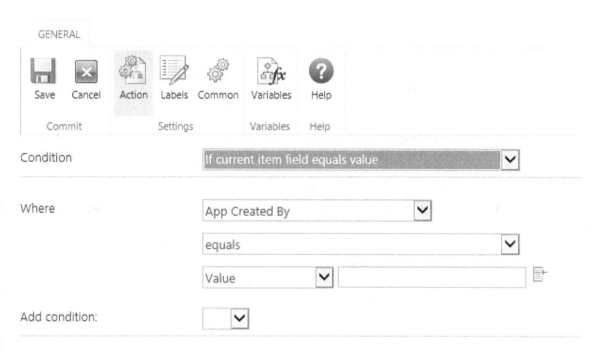

Condition

- If current item field equals value

This condition type evaluates if an individual field of the current item matches or compares to a certain value/column.

- If any value equals value

This condition allows the use of two fields, two workflow variables or two lookups to compare at runtime.

- Title field contains keywords

This condition allows a comparison to be performed that determines if the item's title contains certain specific words.

- Modified in a specific date span

This condition evaluates to true if the current item is modified between two specified dates.

- Modified by a specific person

This condition evaluates to true if the item has been modified by a specific person. The username is case sensitive.

- Person is a valid SharePoint user

This condition checks if the specified user is a member of the SharePoint site.

- Created in a specific date span

This condition checks if the item was created between the specified dates.

- Created by a specific person

This condition checks if an item was created by a specific user.

- The file type is a specific type

This condition checks if the file type extension of the current item is of the specified type.

- The file size is in a specific range kilobytes

This condition checks if the file size of a document is between the specified sizes, in kilobytes.

- Check list item permissions

This condition checks if the permissions of a specified user matches or is higher than the specified permission level provided for an item in a list

- Check list item permission levels

This condition checks if permission levels of a specified user matches or is higher than the permission levels for an item within this list.

These different methods for comparing values are also used in the Filter, Run If and the Set a Condition workflow actions.

The workflow actions contained within the 'Loop' workflow action will be executed for each item for which the condition evaluates to true.

- Run if

This workflow action allows you to execute a group of workflow actions if a set conditions are true. Configuring a 'Run If' workflow action is very similar to configuring a Set a Condition workflow action. The 'Run If' workflow action is a container, if the condition is true all of the workflow actions 'inside' the 'Run If' workflow action will execute. The 'Run If' does not execute any iteration or looping.

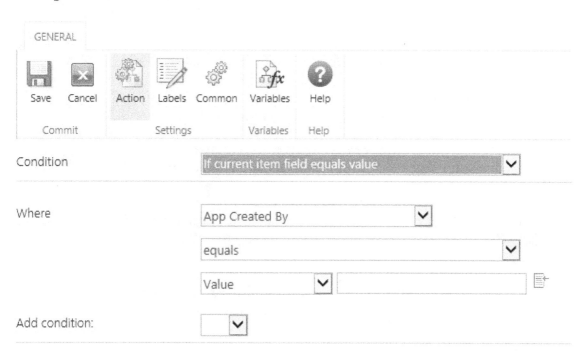

Condition

- If current item field equals value

This condition type evaluates if an individual field of the current item matches or compares to a certain value/column.

- If any value equals value

This condition allows the use of two fields, two workflow variables or two lookups to compare at runtime.

- Title field contains keywords

This condition allows a comparison to be performed that determines if the item's title contains certain specific words.

- Modified in a specific date span

This condition evaluates to true if the current item is modified between two specified dates.

- Modified by a specific person

This condition evaluates to true if the item has been modified by a specific person. The username is case sensitive.

- Person is a valid SharePoint user

This condition checks if the specified user is a member of the SharePoint site.

- Created in a specific date span

This condition checks if the item was created between the specified dates.

- Created by a specific person

This condition checks if an item was created by a specific user.

- The file type is a specific type

This condition checks if the file type extension of the current item is of the specified type.

- The file size is in a specific range kilobytes

This condition checks if the file size of a document is between the specified sizes, in kilobytes.

- Check list item permissions

This condition checks if the permissions of a specified user matches or is higher than the specified permission level provided for an item in a list

- Check list item permission levels

This condition checks if permission levels of a specified user matches or is higher than the permission levels for an item within this list.

- Run Parallel Actions

The 'Run Parallel Actions' workflow action allows you to define multiple execution paths that will all run at the same time. This action does not execute on only one execution path, it executes on all paths simultaneously.

The workflow will not proceed past the 'Run Parallel Actions' workflow action until all branches have completed.

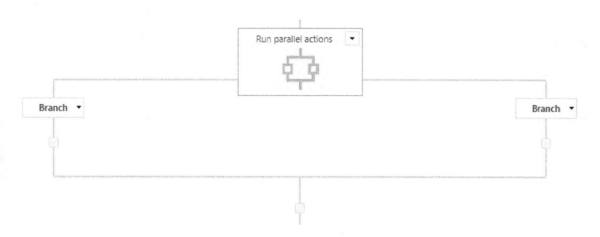

Additional branches can be added either from the action's dropdown menu

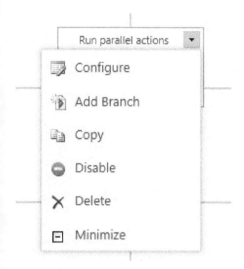

or from any of the 'Branch' drop down menus. The 'Branch' dropdown menus can also be used to move branches right or left within the designer canvas.

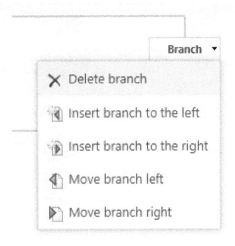

Note on the Configur Action page there are no actual configurations needed.

Configure Action - Run parallel actions

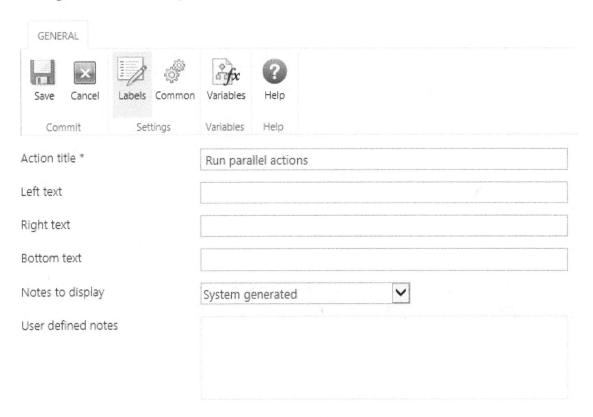

The 'Run Parallel Actions' workflow action does not require configuration, other than defining the Branch structure.

- Set a Condition

This workflow action allows you to execute a group of workflow actions if a set conditions are true. Configuring a 'Set a Condition' is a container similar to the 'Run If' workflow action. The 'Set a Condition' workflow action has 2 execution paths, one path for a true result and one path for a false result

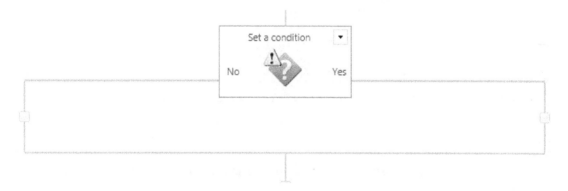

Each Branch - Yes / No - is a container for other workflow actions

Configure Action - Set a condition

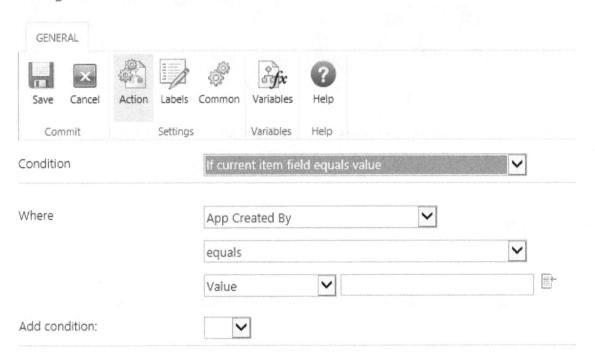

Condition

- **If current item field equals value**
This condition type evaluates if an individual field of the current item matches or compares to a certain value/column.

- **If any value equals value**
This condition allows the use of two fields, two workflow variables or two lookups to compare at runtime.

- **Title field contains keywords**
This condition allows a comparison to be performed that determines if the item's title contains certain specific words.

- **Modified in a specific date span**
This condition evaluates to true if the current item is modified between two specified dates.

- **Modified by a specific person**
This condition evaluates to true if the item has been modified by a specific person. The username is case sensitive.

- Person is a valid SharePoint user

This condition checks if the specified user is a member of the SharePoint site.

- Created in a specific date span

This condition checks if the item was created between the specified dates.

- Created by a specific person

This condition checks if an item was created by a specific user.

- The file type is a specific type

This condition checks if the file type extension of the current item is of the specified type.

- The file size is in a specific range kilobytes

This condition checks if the file size of a document is between the specified sizes, in kilobytes.

- Check list item permissions

This condition checks if the permissions of a specified user matches or is higher than the specified permission level provided for an item in a list

- Check list item permission levels

This condition checks if permission levels of a specified user matches or is higher than the permission levels for an item within this list.

- Switch

The 'Switch' workflow action allows you to define multiple execution based upon a list field's value

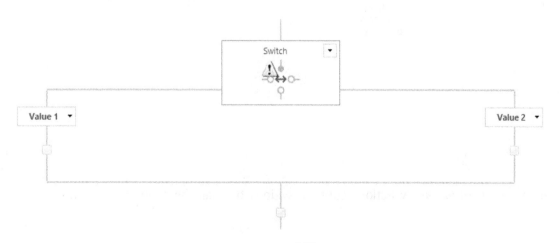

Branch names can be modified and additional branches can be added to make the visual display more representative of what is actually being evaluated.

In the configuration example below the 'Approval Status' column is being evaluated. This 'Switch' workflow action has three execution paths, one for each of the following possible values for the 'Approval Status' column:

Approved

Rejected

Pending

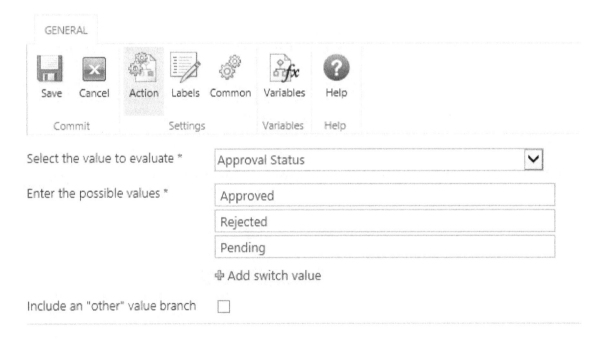

Operations

The Operations group of workflow actions contains actions that can be thought of as utility operations.

- Build String

This workflow action allows you to build and manipulate strings of characters and store the result in a workflow variable

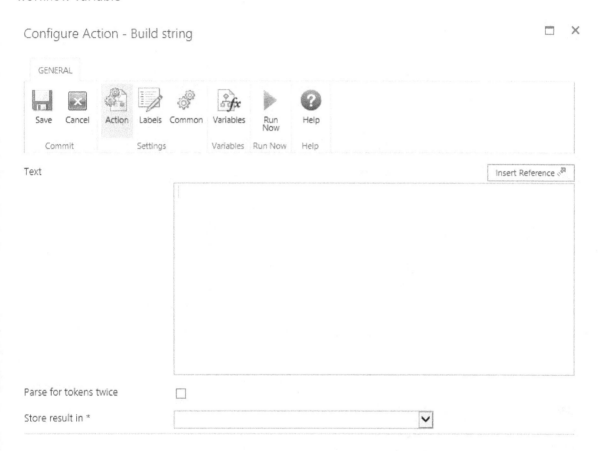

Using the Insert Reference functionality it is possible to construct very dynamic and useful strings

- Calculate Date

The Calculate Date workflow action allows you to create a new date value by adding or subtracting from an existing date value.

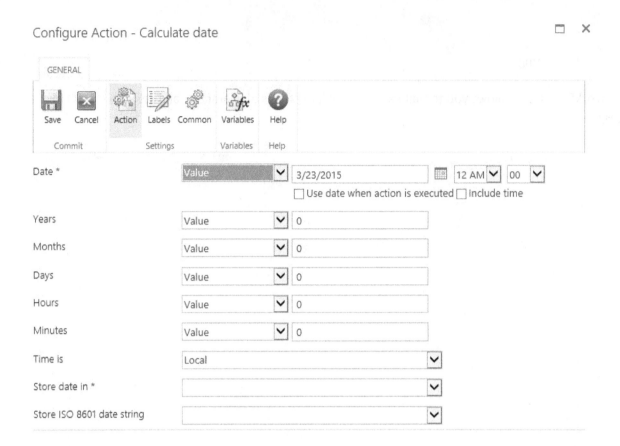

Date

The date to use as a base for the calculation can be:

A specific date

A lookup from a variable or list

The current date.

- Collection Operation

The Collection Operation workflow action allows you execute operations to read and modify the contents of a Collection workflow variable.

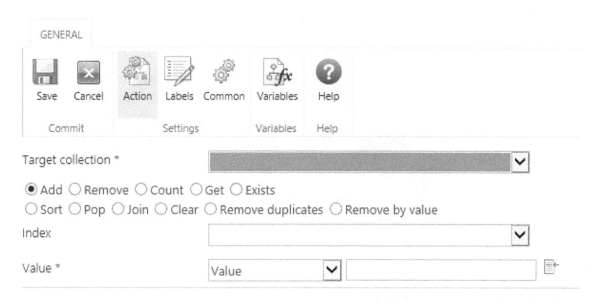

Target Collection

The Collection workflow variable

- Convert Value

The Convert Value workflow action allows you to convert an existing workflow variable value from one type to another

Configure Action - Convert value

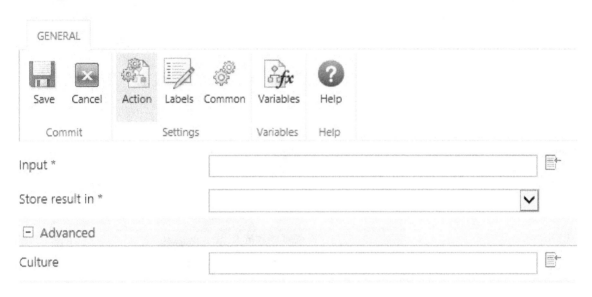

Input

The workflow value that will be converted

Store result in

The workflow variable the result (converted) value will be stored in

Culture

Specify the language information CLID

- End Workflow

Use this workflow action to terminate the workflow.

Configure Action - End workflow

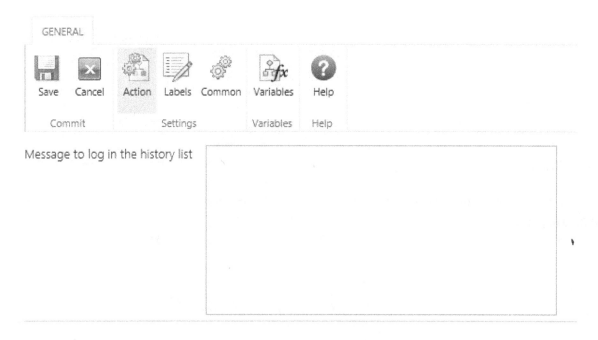

Optionally you can write a comment to the workflow history log upon termination.

- Log in History List

Use this workflow action to write a comment to the workflow history log

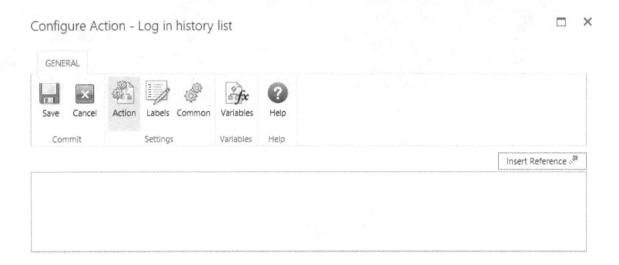

- Math Operation

The Math Operation workflow action allows you to perform basic calculations and store the result in a workflow variable.

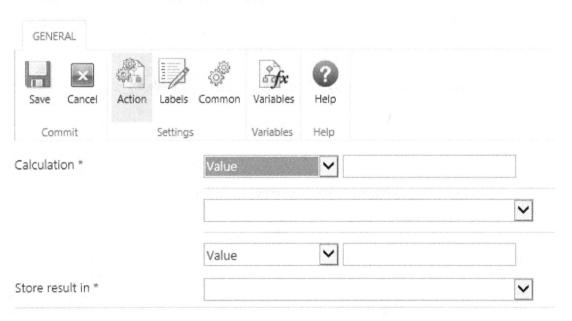

Calculation

- Plus
- Minus
- Divided by
- Multiplied by
- Modulus

Store result in

The workflow variable to store the result of the calculation

- Pause For...

Use this workflow action to pause execution of the workflow for a defined period of time

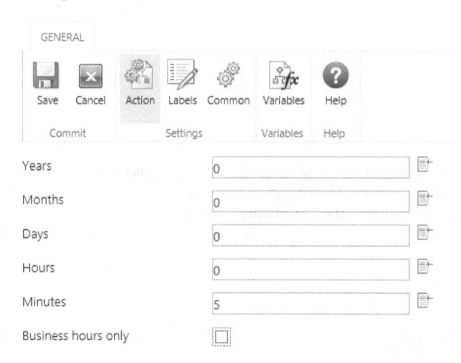

You can define the pause to last for any combination of Years, Months, Days, Hours, or Minutes

- Pause Until...

Use this workflow action to pause the execution of a workflow until a specified date and time.

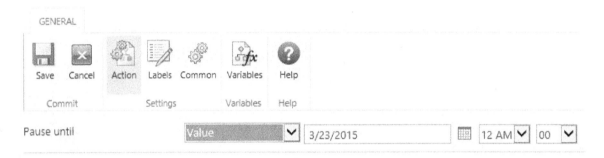

- Regular Expression

Use this workflow action to perform a regular expression on a block of text. A regular expression is a pattern of characters. Regular expressions can be used to check to see if an input value matches a pattern or it can be used to replace input characters that match a pattern with other characters.

Configure Action - Regular expression

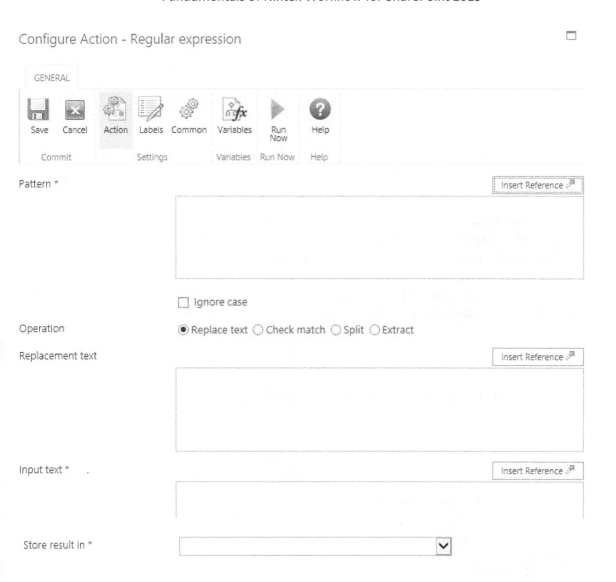

Pattern

The regular expression pattern to apply to the text.

This action uses the Microsoft .NET regular expression syntax.

Ignore case

Use this option to specify that the pattern should be treated as case insensitive.

Operation

- Replace text replaces the text matching the pattern with the replacement text.
- Check match outputs a yes/no value to indicate if the input text matches the pattern.
- Split divides the input text into sections using the pattern as a delimiter. The output value is a collection containing each portion of the split text.
- Extract searches the input text for sub strings that match the pattern. Each matching substring is stored in the collection output value.

Input text

The input text to which the regular expression will be applied.

Store result in

The workflow variable the result will be stored in

- Store Data

Use this workflow action to save data that can be accessed by other workflow instances using the Retrieve Data workflow action. This is very useful when you want one instance of a running workflow to interact in some way with other instances of a running workflow.

Configure Action - Store data

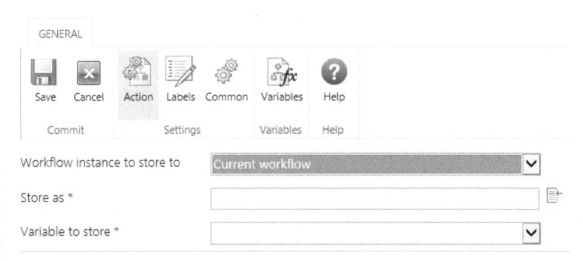

Workflow instance to store to

Current Workflow

Workflow Variable equal to the instance ID

Store as

The name this value will be stored as. When using the Retrieve Data action this name will be used to retrieve the value.

Variable to store

The workflow variable whose value will be stored.

- Retrieve Data

Use this workflow action to retrieve data that has been stored using the Store Data workflow action.

Configure Action - Retrieve data

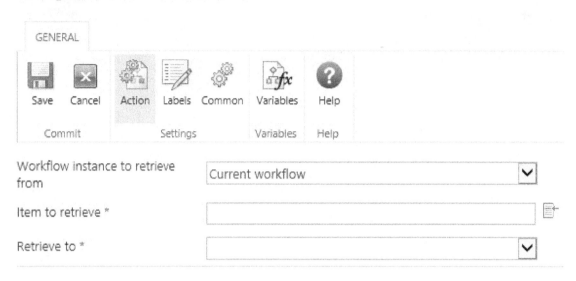

Workflow instance to retrieve from

Current Workflow

Workflow Variable equal to the instance ID

Item to Retrieve

The name this value to be retrieved.

Retrieve To

The workflow variable the value will be stored in.

- Set Variable

Use this workflow action to set or edit the value of a workflow variable

Configure Action - Set variable

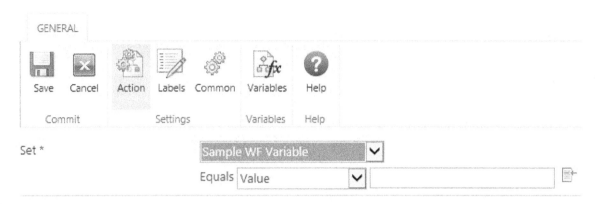

Set

Select the workflow variable whose value you would like to change

- Set Workflow Status

Use this workflow action to set the status of the current workflow

Configure Action - Set workflow status

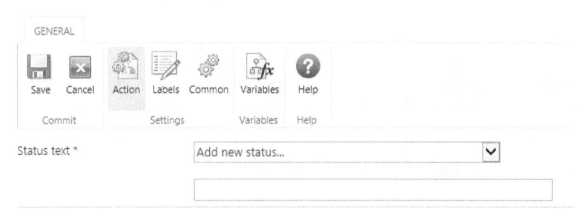

Status text

You can select a status that has been previously created or create a new status

- Start Workflow

Use this workflow action to start a workflow instance.

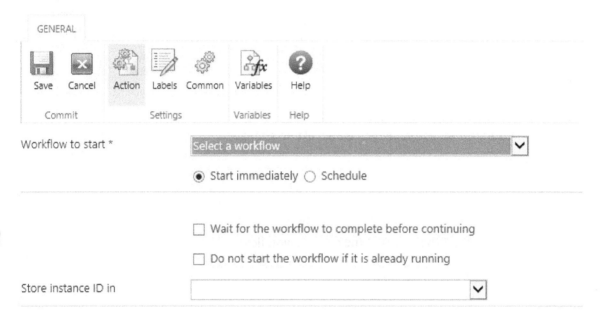

Workflow to start

Select which workflow to start, by selecting a workflow name. You can start either a Site Workflow or another workflow associated with the current list or library.

Store instance ID in

The workflow variable you will store the Instance ID of the newly started workflow in

- Terminate Workflow

Use this workflow to terminate any running or error-ed workflow on the current item.

Configure Action - Terminate workflow

Stop workflow

All except current workflow

Stop Workflow

All except current workflow

Any named workflow on the current list or library (or site for a site workflow)

- Wait for Check Out Status Change

Use this workflow action to cause the workflow execution to pause until the Check Out Status changes for the current document

Configure Action - Wait for check out status change

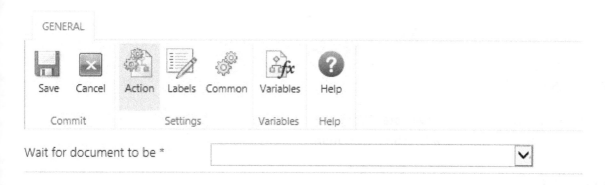

Wait for document to be *

Wait for document to be

Checked out

Checked in

Unlocked by document editor

Discarded

- Wait for Item Update

Use this workflow action to pause execution of the current workflow until an item is updated to a specified value.

Wait for

Select the column and a value to evaluate. When the selected column has been updated to the designated value the workflow will resume execution.

Provisioning

The Provisioning group contains workflow actions that work with user (Active Directory) objects and site objects.

- Add user to AD group

Use this workflow action to add an Active Directory to an Active Directory security group

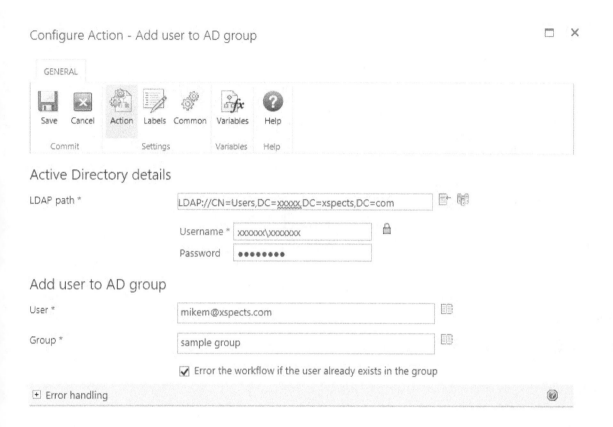

LDAP Path

Enter the LDAP path to the Active Directory domain or use the LDAP picker tool to choose the domain which will write out the LDAP path for you

You must enter the credentials of an account with sufficient permissions to read Active Directory

LDAP Picker

Active Directory details

LDAP path *

LDAP://CN=Users,DC=xxxxx,DC=xspects,   Add Domain

Username *

Password

User

Select the user you wish to add to the Active directory group

Group

Select the Active Directory group you wish to add the selected user to

- Compile audience

Use this workflow action to compile an existing audience within the SharePoint farm.

Configure Action - Compile audience

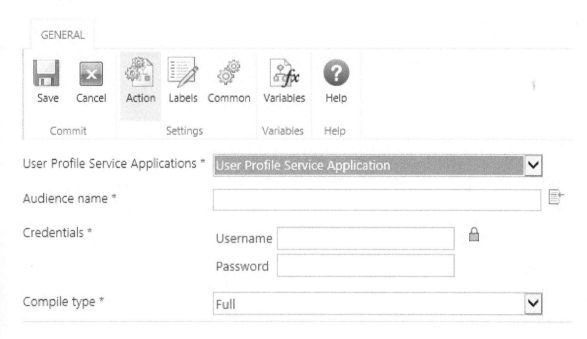

User Profile Service Application

Select the User Profile Service Application which hosts the audience you wish to compile

Audience name

Select the audience you wish to compile

Credentials

Enter the username and password of an account with sufficient permissions to compile the audience

Compile Type

Full

Incremental

- Create AD group

User this workflow action to create an Active Directory group

Configure Action - Create AD group

GENERAL

| Save | Cancel | Action | Labels | Common | Variables | Help |

| Commit | | | Settings | | Variables | Help |

Active Directory details

LDAP path *

Username *

Password

Group details

Group scope *
- ○ Domain local
- ○ Global
- ○ Universal

Group type *
- ○ Security
- ○ Distribution

Group name *

LDAP Path

Enter the LDAP path to the Active Directory domain or use the LDAP picker tool to choose the domain which will write out the LDAP path for you

You must enter the credentials of an account with sufficient permissions to read Active Directory

LDAP Picker

Active Directory details

LDAP path *   LDAP://CN=Users,DC=xxxxx,DC=xspects,   Add Domain

Username *

Password

Group Scope

Domain Local

Global

Universal

Group Type

Security

Distribution

Group Name

A name for the new group

- Create AD user

Use this workflow action to create a new Active Directory user

Configure Action - Create AD user

GENERAL

Save	Cancel	Action	Labels	Common	Variables	Help
Commit			Settings		Variables	Help

Where the account will be created

LDAP path *

Username *

Password

New account details

sAMAccountName *

Common name *

User principal name

Example: user@domain.com

Display name		
Given name		
Last name		
Email		
Manager		

New account password

Generate password	☐	
New password		

Other fields

Fields	Please select ▾	Add

LDAP Path

Enter the LDAP path to the Active Directory domain or use the LDAP picker tool to choose the domain which will write out the LDAP path for you

You must enter the credentials of an account with sufficient permissions to read Active Directory

LDAP Picker

Active Directory details

LDAP path *	LDAP://CN=Users,DC=xxxxx,DC=xspects,	Add Domain
Username *		
Password		

sAMAccountName

A unique username for the Active new Directory user. This must be a unique value.

Common Name

The Active Directory Common Name value. This must be unique within the Container in which it will be created.

User Principal Name

The display name of the principal user. If this field is left blank, it will default to the value of sAMAAccountName@domain.com

Additional User Account Properties as needed

- Create audience

Use this workflow action to create a new SharePoint audience within the current farm

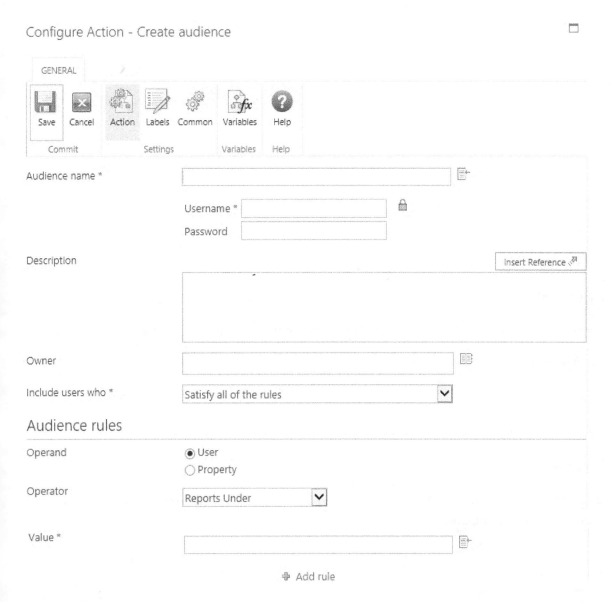

Audience Name

The name of the new audience

You must provide credentials of a user account with sufficient permissions to create an audience in the SharePoint farm

Description

A description of the new audience

Owner

The user account designated as the audience owner

Include users who

Define which users will be included in the audience when multiple rules are used to define the audience:

Satisfy all the rules

Satisfy any of the rules

Audience rules

Audience rules define what users are memebers of the audience. Mulitple rules can be created, a minimum of one rule is required.

- Create site

Use this workflow action to create a new SharePoint site within the current SharePoint farm.

Configure Action - Create site

GENERAL

Save	Cancel	Action	Labels	Common	Variables	Help

Commit   Settings   Variables   Help

Title *

Description

Inherit permissions   ✔

Parent site *   ⦿ Select a parent site ◯ Enter a URL

Select team site

URL name *

Template *

Display on the Quick Launch of the parent site

Display on the top link bar of the parent site

Use top link bar from the parent site

Store URL in

☐ Override credentials

Credentials   Username

             Password

Title

The title of the new SharePoint site

Description

A description of the new SharePoint site

Inherit Permissions

Yes/No - Defines whether the new site will have unique permissions or inherit permissions for its parent site

Parent Site

The new site must be a child of a current Site Collection. Either select one using the graphical interface or enter a URL

URL name

Template

Display on the Quick Launch of the Parent Site

Display on the Top Link Bar of the Parent Site

Use the Top Link Bar from the Parent Site

Store URL in

- Create site collection

Use this workflow action to create a new Site Collection

Configure Action - Create site collection

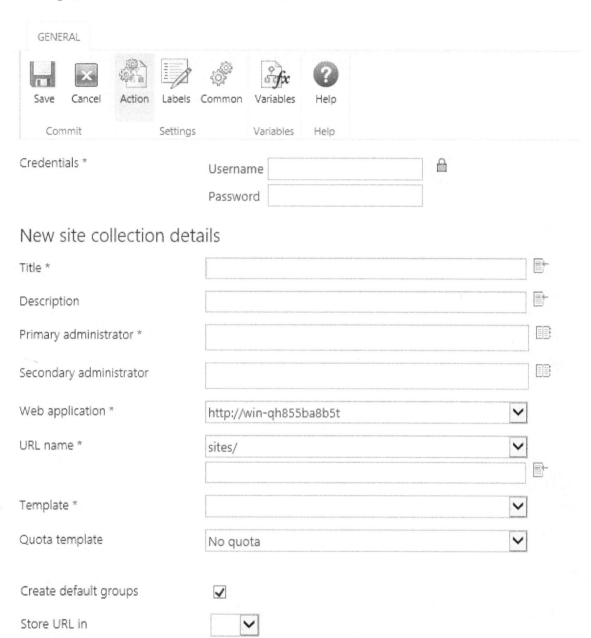

Credentials

Username and password of a user account with sufficient permissions to create a new site collection.

Description

A description of the site collection

Primary Site Administrator

A user who will be a site collection administrator - required

Secondary Site Administrator

Another user who will be a site collection administrator - optional

Web Application

The web application that will host the new site collection

URL Name

The URL of the top level site of the new site collection. This defines where the new site collection will exist within the web application. Options are based upon defined managed paths for the web application.

Template

The site template to use to create the top level site of the new site collection

Quota Template

Select the site quota to use when creating the new site collection

Create Default Groups

Yes / No

Store Url in

The workflow variable to store the url of the new site collection in

- Decommission AD user

The Decommission AD user workflow action allows you to disable or delete an Active Directory user

Configure Action - Decommission AD user

GENERAL

Save	Cancel	Action	Labels	Common	Variables	Help
Commit		Settings			Variables	Help

Active Directory details

LDAP path *

Username *

Password

Decommission user

User *

Action *   ● Disable ○ Delete

LDAP Path

Enter the LDAP path to the Active Directory domain or use the LDAP picker tool 📖 to choose the domain which will write out the LDAP path for you

You must enter the credentials of an account with sufficient permissions to edit Active Directory

LDAP Picker

Active Directory details

LDAP path *   LDAP://CN=Users,DC=xxxxx,DC=xspects,   Add Domain

Username * [   ] 🔒

Password [   ]

User

Select the user you wish to either disable or delete. Enter the sAMAccountName of the user.

Action

Disable

Delete

- Decommission site collection

Use this action to alter the state of or delete a site collection.

Configure Action - Decommission site collection

GENERAL

Save	Cancel	Action	Labels	Common	Variables	Help

Commit		Settings		Variables	Help

Credentials *   Username [   ] 🔒

                       Password [   ]

Site collection details

URL *   [   ]

Decommission options

Action *   [Read only ∨]

Reason *   [   ]

Credentials

Enter the username and password of a user account with sufficient permissions to delete a site collection.

URL

The URL of the site collection to be decommisioned

Action

Read only

No Access

Delete

Reason

The reason for decommissioning the site collection

- Delete AD group

Use this workflow action to delete an Active Directory security or distribution group

Configure Action - Delete AD group

LDAP Path

Enter the LDAP path to the Active Directory domain or use the LDAP picker tool to choose the domain which will write out the LDAP path for you

You must enter the credentials of an account with sufficient permissions to read Active Directory

LDAP Picker

Active Directory details

LDAP path *   LDAP://CN=Users,DC=xxxxx,DC=xspects,   [Add Domain]

Username *

Password

Group Name

The name of the group to be deleted

- Delete audience

Use this workflow action to delete a SharePoint audience

Configure Action - Delete audience

Audience name *

Username *

Password

Audience Name

The name of the SharePoint audience to be deleted. You must enter the username and password of a user account with sufficient permissions to delete an audience.

- Delete site

Use this workflow action to delete a SharePoint site (along with any sub-sites)

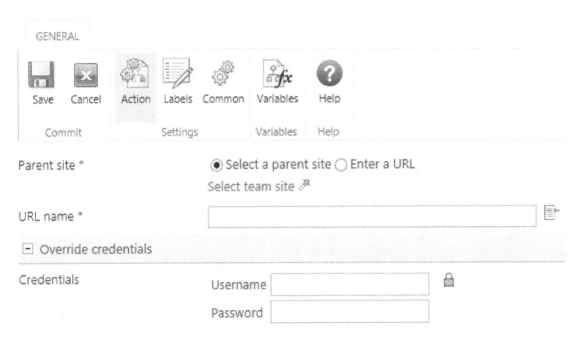

Parent Site

Either select a parent site or enter the URL to a parent site. The parent site can be the site you want to delete.

URL Name

The url to the site to be deleted, releative to the parent site. Do not enter the full URL. If the site to be delete is the parent site, enter a forward slash for the URL name (/).

- Enable Lync / OCS

Use this workflow action to enable Lync or Office Communications Server for a specific Active Directory account

Configure Action - Enable Lync / OCS

GENERAL

| Save | Cancel | Action | Labels | Common | Variables | Help |

| Commit | | | Settings | | Variables | Help |

Server version   Lync 2010 / 2013 ▼

Lync Details

Lync server *

Username *

Password

Registrar pool *

Account to enable *

SIP address

Telephony

Telephony   Audio/video disabled ⌄

Policies

Conferencing policy   [   ] 📄

Client version policy   [   ] 📄

PIN policy   [   ] 📄

External access policy   [   ] 📄

Archiving policy   [   ] 📄

Location policy   [   ] 📄

Client policy   [   ] 📄

[−] Advanced

Domain controller   [   ] 📄

SIP address type   [   ] 📄

SIP domain   [   ] 📄

Authentication mode   Default ⌄

Server Version

Select the version of Lync or OCS

Lync Server

The name of the Lync Server. You must provide the username and password of a user account with sufficient permissions on the Lync server

Registrar Pool

The FQDN of the Registrar pool where the users' Lync Server account will be honed.

Account to enable

The sAMAccountName of the Active Directory account to activate

SIP address

The SIP address for the Active Directory Account

Telephony

Select the desired communication type.
AV
PC to PC
Enterprise Voice
Remote Call Control
Remote Call Control Only

Conferencing policy

The conferencing policy specifies the conferencing experience for participants.

Client version policy

The client version policy checks the SIP User Agent header to determine the client version.

PIN policy

The PIN policy provides a personal identification number (PIN) authentication to users with IP phones.

External access policy

Communicate with users who have SIP accounts with a federated organization

Communicate with users who have SIP accounts with a public instant messaging Access Microsoft Lync Server 2010/2013 over the internet, without having to log on to your internal network.

Archiving policy

The archiving policy controls whether archiving for specific users is enabled or disabled for internal and external communications.

Location policy

The location policy automatically locates clients within a network.

Client policy

The client policy determines the features made available to users.

Domain controller

Connect to the specified domain controller in order to enable a user account

SP address type

Instructs Lync Server to auto-generate a SIP address for the new user.

- Provision user in Exchange

Use this action to create a new mailbox in Microsoft Exchange for a selected Active Directory user account. A Nintex Workflow Exchange Connector Service must be installed to Provision a user in Exchange.

Configure Action - Provision user in Exchange

GENERAL

| Save | Cancel | Action | Labels | Common | Variables | Help |

| Commit | | | Settings | | Variables | Help |

Exchange connector service

Web service URL *

Username *

Password

Provision details

Version *   Exchange 2003 ▾

Mailbox container *

User *

Web Service URL

The path to the Nintex Workflow Exchange Connector Service.

For example (http://www.mycompany.com/siteECS/EmailProvisioning.asmx)

You must provide the username and password that were created in the prerequisite section of the Nintex Workflow Exchange Connector Service installation manual

Version

The version of Microsoft Exchange you are using

Mailbox Container

The LDAP path to the Mailbox container the new mailbox will be created in

User

The Active Directory user account to create a new mailbox for

- Remove user from AD group

Use this workflow action to remove an Active Directory user from and Active Directory group

Configure Action - Remove user from AD group

GENERAL

Save	Cancel	Action	Labels	Common	Variables	Help
Commit			Settings		Variables	Help

Active Directory details

LDAP path *

Username

Password

Remove user from AD group

User *

Group *

LDAP Path

Enter the LDAP path to the Active Directory domain or use the LDAP picker tool [image] to choose the domain which will write out the LDAP path for you

You must enter the credentials of an account with sufficient permissions to read Active Directory

LDAP Picker

Active Directory details

LDAP path * | LDAP://CN=Users,DC=xxxxx,DC=xspects, | Add Domain

Username *   [   ] 🔒

Password   [   ]

User

The Active Directory user account you wish to remove from the selected group

Group

The Active Directory group you wish to remove the user from

- Update AD user

Use the Update AD User workflow action to modify the attributes or properties of an Active Directory user account

Configure Action - Update AD user

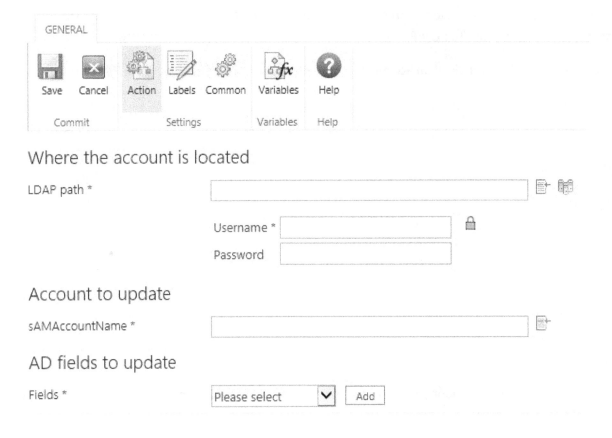

Where the account is located

LDAP path *

Username *

Password

Account to update

sAMAccountName *

AD fields to update

Fields *   Please select ⌄   Add

LDAP Path

Enter the LDAP path to the Active Directory domain or use the LDAP picker tool to choose the domain which will write out the LDAP path for you

You must enter the credentials of an account with sufficient permissions to read Active Directory

LDAP Picker

Active Directory details

LDAP path * | LDAP://CN=Users,DC=xxxxx,DC=xspects, | Add Domain |

Username * [   ] 🔒

Password [   ]

sAMAccountName

The Active Directory user whose properties will be changed

Fields

The attributes or properties to be changed, and their new values

- Update user profile

Use this workflow action to update a SharePoint user's SharePoint profile

Configure Action - Update user profile

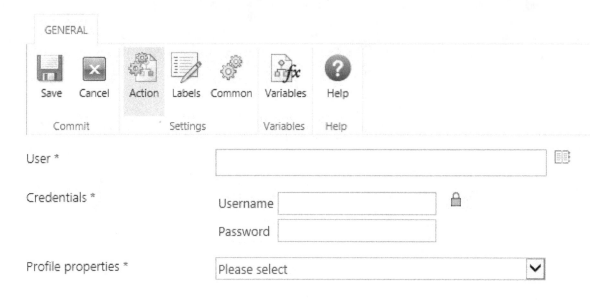

User

Select the SharePoint user whose properties you wish to change

Credentials

Enter credentials of a user account with sufficent permissions to edit user profile properties

Profile Properties

Select the user profile properties you wish to change

User Interaction

The user interaction group contains workflow actions that generally request some activity on the part of a SharePoint user, such as assigning tasks to users.

- Assign Flexi Task

The Assign Flexi Task workflow action is one of the most commonly used in Nintex Workflows. The Flexi Task is used in lieu of the standard SharePoint task assignment which can be accomplished with the Assign To-Do Task. The Assign Flexi Task workflow action contains a number of improvements over the Assign To-Do Task.

The Assign Flexi Task workflow action creates an action with at least two execution paths - Approve and Reject

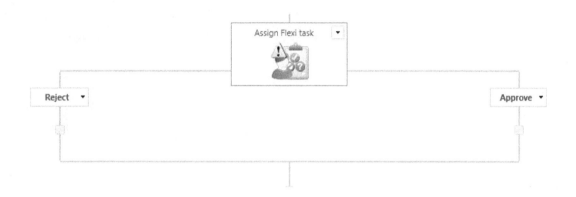

Different workflow actions can be placed within each execution path.

The positions of each branch (relative to each other) can be changed using the branch dropdown menu

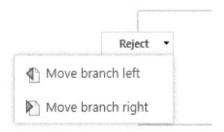

Configure Action - Assign Flexi task

GENERAL

Save	Cancel	Action	Task Notification	Not Required Notification	Reminders	Escalation	Edit Task Form	Labels	Common	Variables	Help
Commit					Settings					Variables	Help

Assignees *

☐ Create individual tasks for all group members

Allow delegation   ☐

Allow LazyApproval   ☐ (only applicable with email delivery)

Task description   Insert Reference

Outcomes   📝 Approve ✕
                            📝 Reject ✕
                            ➕ Add outcome

Behaviour	● First response applies	○ Majority decides
	○ Majority must choose a specific outcome	○ All must agree
	○ All must agree on a specific outcome	

Store outcome in	[▼]
Store outcome achieved in	[▼]
Task name	Workflow task
Task content type	Nintex Workflow Multi Outcome Task ▼
Priority	(2) Normal
Due Date	Value ▼ [ ] 🔲
Form type	Default ▼
Store task IDs in	[▼]

⊟ Item permissions

Set user permissions to	Unchanged ▼
When task is complete, set user permissions to	Unchanged ▼

⊟ Advanced Options

☐ Do not create branches
☐ Include an 'Other' branch to capture outcomes not listed in the Outcomes section
☐ Do not use LazyApproval terms when interpreting email responses

Assignees

The users or groups who will be assigned the task. A task can be assigned to a single user or multiple users. If a task is assigned to multiple users explicitly (by listing each user) each user will have a task assigned to them individually. If a task is assigned only to a group one task will be assigned to that group. Any member of the group will be able to complete the task.

If the Create individual task for group members box is selected an individual task will be created and assigned to each member of the group.

223

Allow Delegation

Yes/No - Choose whether the assignee can delegate the task (or assign the task) to another person or group.

Allow LazyApproval

Yes/No - Choose whether the LazyApproval will be available to assignees.

The LazyApproval option allows assignees to complete their assigned task (either approving or rejecting) simply by replying to a Nintex generated email or OCS / Lync message.

The LazyApproval is only available when both incoming and outgoing email are configured within the SharePoint farm.

When you receive an email indicating that a task has been assigned to you, simply reply to the email with a single word to either approve or reject the task.

The email response should be a single word (of a set of mapped words). All responses must map to either Approve or Deny. The table below shows the default Lazy Approval phrases and the outcome they map to:

Phrase	Outcome
approve	Approve
approved	Approve
decline	Deny
declined	Deny
no	Deny
ok	Approve
reject	Deny
rejected	Deny
yes	Approve

Task Description

Provide a longer description of the task being assigned.

Outcomes

The **Outcomes** define all the possible responses to the task. By default there are two possible outcomes:

- Approve
- Reject

Each Outcome is also a branch on the workflow action. Each branch has its own set of actions to control workflow execution.

Outcomes can be added by clicking the *Add outcome* link

If an Outcome is added, such as in the example below, a branch is added as well:

Behavior

Behaviors define what Nintex will do when a task has more than one assignee.

If the task is assigned to one person things are pretty simple, that person's response will apply - if they Approve the task it is approved, if they Reject the task it is rejected.

What if there are 2 approvers? Or 4 approvers?

You define what should happen by defining the behaviors. There are 5 basic alternatives (or behaviors) to define what should happen when multiple approvers are assigned:

- First Response Applies - Pretty simple here, the first assigned approver to respond decides the issue. If the first response is Approved the task is approved, if the first response is Rejected the task is rejected.
- Majority Must Choose a Specific Outcome - The majority of assignees MUST agree on a chosen outcome. If a majority does not agree on the chosen outcome the *Outcome Achieved* variable is set to *No*. The overall task outcome will not be set, it will be blank. In the case of 4 approvers with a 2 -2 tie, there would not be an outcome.
- All Must Agree on a Specific Outcome - All assignees MUST agree on a chosen outcome. If All do not agree on that outcome the *Outcome Achieved* variable is set to *No*. The overall task outcome will not be set, it will be blank.
- Majority Decides - Whichever outcome is selected by the majority will be selected as the outcome. If a majority does not agree on an outcome the *Outcome Achieved In* variable is set to *No*. The overall task outcome will not be set, it will be blank. In the case of 4 approvers with a 2 - 2 tie, there would not be an outcome.

Store Outcome In

The Outcome Achieved will be stored in this workflow variable

Store Outcome Achieved In

This is a Yes/No variable that is used to indicate if an Outcome was Achieved

Task Name

The title of the task. This title appears in the Workflow Task list for the task created.

Task Content Type

The content type of the task item created in the Workflow Task list

Priority

Select the Priority of the task created in the Workflow Task list

Due Date

The Task due date

Form Type

- Default
- Nintex
- InfoPath

Item Permissions

Allows you to set the user permission on the new task item, or leave them unchanged.

When task is complete, set user permissions to

Allows you to set the user permission on the new task item after the task has been completed, or leave them unchanged.

This can often be used when you want to make something read only after it has been completed.

Task Notification Tab

When a task is assigned to a user an email notification is sent to the assigned users. The Notification tab contains properties defining the notification email.

The email message can be modified, but the default is:

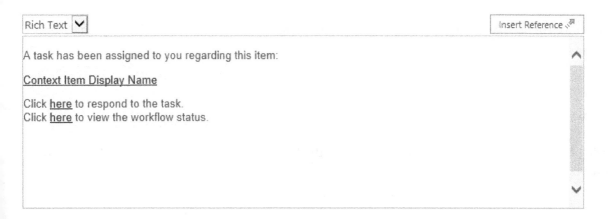

Configure Action - Assign Flexi task

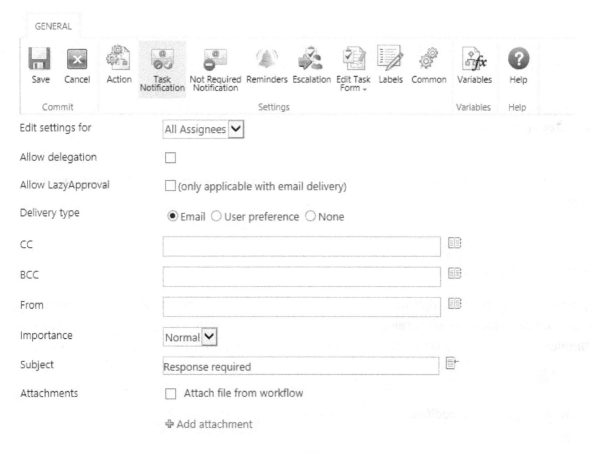

Edit settings for

Allows you to define specific edit settings for a specific assignee (assuming the task is assigned to more than one assignee)

Allow Delegation

Yes/No - Choose whether the assignee can delegate the task (or assign the task) to another person or group.

Allow LazyApproval

Yes/No - Choose whether the LazyApproval will be available to assignees.

Delivery Type

- None
- Email
- SMS / OCS/ Lync

The notification will automatically go to the assignees. You can also select CC and BCC recipients of the notification.

Not Required Notification Tab

When a task is assigned to multiple users and is completed before all users respond, those assignees who have not yet responded will receive an email notifying them that they do not need to do anything. The Notification not Required tab contains properties defining the notification email.

The email message can be modified, but the default is:

Configure Action - Assign Flexi task

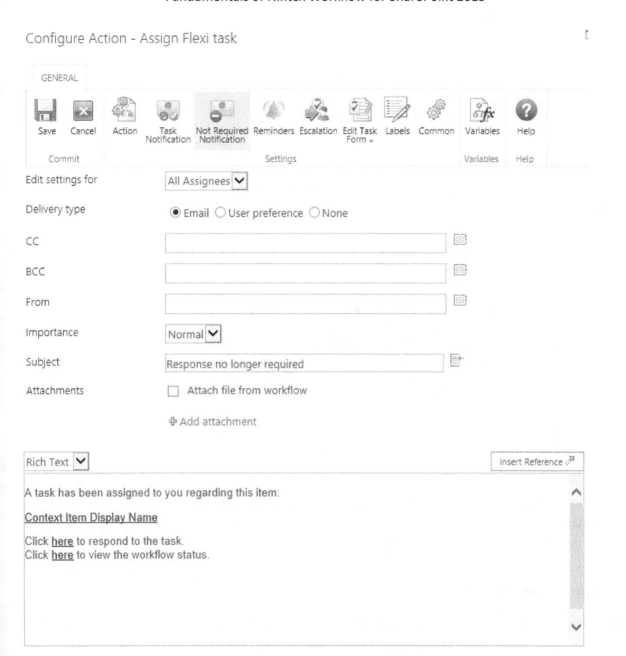

Edit settings for

Allows you to define specific edit settings for a specific assignee (assuming the task is assigned to more than one assignee)

Allow Delegation

Yes/No - Choose whether the assignee can delegate the task (or assign the task) to another person or group.

Allow LazyApproval

Yes/No - Choose whether the LazyApproval will be available to assignees.

Delivery Type

- None
- Email
- SMS / OCS/ Lync

The notification will automatically go to the assignees. You can also select CC and BCC recipients of the notification.

Reminders Notification Tab

When a task is assigned you can define reminders, which are additional notifications sent to assignees who have not completed the task within a defined time period.

Configure Action - Assign Flexi task

GENERAL

| Save | Cancel | Action | Task Notification | Not Required Notification | Reminders | Escalation | Edit Task Form | Labels | Common | Variables | Help |

Commit   Settings   Variables   Help

Number of reminders   [0]

Time between reminders

     Days: [0]

     Hours: [0]

     Mins: [0]

Time calculation

     ☐ During business days only

     ☐ During business hours only

CC   [ ]

BCC   [ ]

From   [ ]

Importance   [Normal ▼]

Subject   [ ]

Attach file   ☐

[Rich Text ▼]   [Insert Reference ↗]

A task has been assigned to you regarding this item:

Context Item Display Name

Click here to respond to the task.
Click here to view the workflow status.

Number of reminders

The number of reminders to be sent

Time between reminders

Time calculation

Specifies whether or not hours outside the work week should be included when counting down to send a reminder.

During business days only

The During business days only option will specify that weekends or holidays are not included in the countdown.

During business hours only

The During business hours only option specifies that only business hours are used in the count down.

Escalation Notification Tab

When a task is assigned but is not completed Escalation rules can be defined to deal with un-completed tasks.

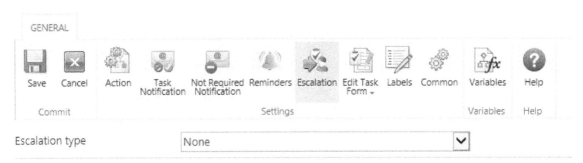

Escalation options are

- Delegate Task
- Complete Task

- Assign To-Do Task

This workflow action will assign a SharePoint task to one or more users.

Configure Action - Assign to-do task

GENERAL										
💾 Save	✖ Cancel	Action	Task Notification	Not Required Notification	Reminders	Escalation	Labels	Common	Variables	❓ Help
Commit				Settings					Variables	Help

Assignees *

☐ Create individual tasks for all group members

Allow delegation   ☑

Task description   Insert Reference ↗

Task options
- ⦿ All must respond
- ○ First response applies

Content type *   ○ Use existing   ⦿ Create new

Due Date   Value ▾ [   ] 🗓

Store task IDs in   [   ] ▾

⊟ **Item permissions**

Set user permissions to   Unchanged ▾

When task is complete, set user permissions to   Unchanged ▾

Assignees

The users or groups who will be assigned the task. A task can be assigned to a single user or multiple users. If a task is assigned to multiple users explicitly (by listing each user) each user will have a task assigned to them individually. If a task is assigned only to a group one task will be assigned to that group. Any member of the group will be able to complete the task.

If the Create individual task for group members box is selected an individual task will be created and assigned to each member of the group.

Allow Delegation

Yes/No - Choose whether the assignee can delegate the task (or assign the task) to another person or group.

Task Description

A description of the task.

Task Options (Behaviors)

All Must Respond

All assignees must respond and complete the task

First Response Applies

Only one assignee must respond and complete the task

Content Type

The content type of the task item created in the Workflow Task list

Due Date

The Task due date

Store Task IDs In

The workflow variable to store the value of the ID of the new task item

Item Permissions

Allows you to set the user permission on the new task item, or leave them unchanged.

When task is complete, set user permissions to

Allows you to set the user permission on the new task item after the task has been completed, or leave them unchanged.

This can often be used when you want to make something read only after it has been completed.

Task Notification Tab

When a task is assigned to a user an email notification is sent to the assigned users. The Notification tab contains properties defining the notification email.

The email message can be modified, but the default is:

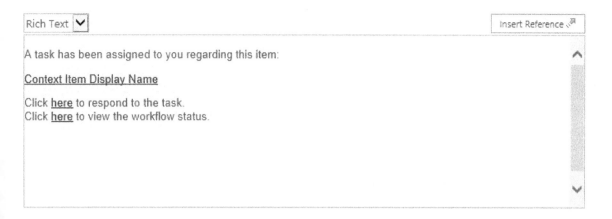

Configure Action - Assign to-do task

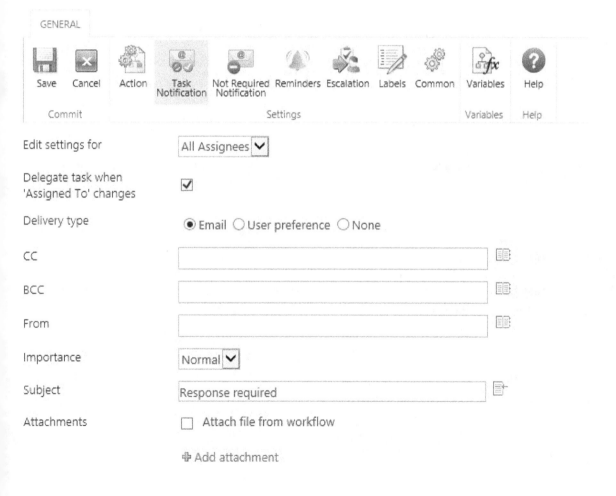

Edit settings for

Allows you to define specific edit settings for a specific assignee (assuming the task is assigned to more than one assignee)

Delegate task when 'Assigned To' changes

Yes/No - Choose whether the task will be when it is reassigned.

Delivery Type

- None
- Email
- SMS / OCS/ Lync

The notification will automatically go to the assignees. You can also select CC and BCC recipients of the notification.

Not Required Notification Tab

When a task is assigned to multiple users and is completed before all users respond, those assignees who have not yet responded will receive an email notifying them that they do not need to do anything. The Notification not Required tab contains properties defining the notification email.

The email message can be modified, but the default is:

Configure Action - Assign to-do task

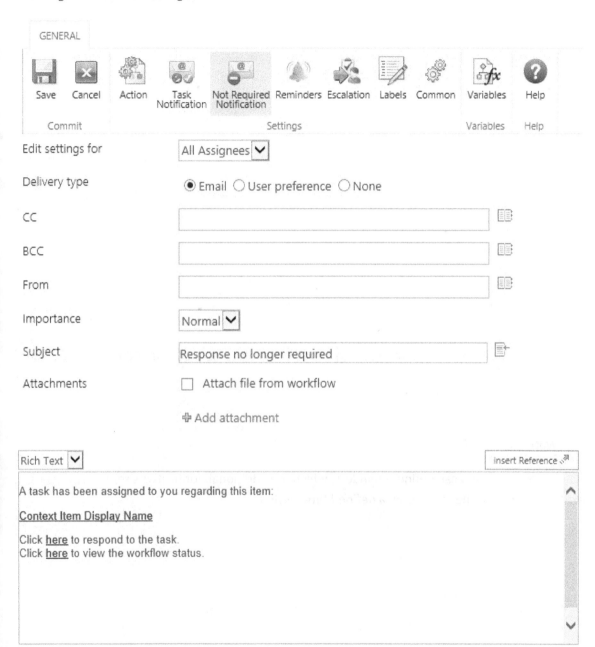

Edit settings for

Allows you to define specific edit settings for a specific assignee (assuming the task is assigned to more than one assignee)

Delivery Type

- None
- Email
- SMS / OCS/ Lync

The notification will automatically go to the assignees. You can also select CC and BCC recipients of the notification.

Reminders Notification Tab

When a task is assigned you can define reminders, which are additional notifications sent to assignees who have not completed the task within a defined time period.

Configure Action - Assign to-do task

GENERAL

Save	Cancel	Action	Task Notification	Not Required Notification	Reminders	Escalation	Labels	Common	Variables	Help

Commit	Settings	Variables	Help

Number of reminders | 0

Time between reminders

Days: 0

Hours: 0

Mins: 0

Time calculation

☐ During business days only
☐ During business hours only

CC

BCC

From

Importance | Normal ⌄

Subject

Attach file ☐

Rich Text ⌄   Insert Reference

A task has been assigned to you regarding this item:

Context Item Display Name

Click here to respond to the task.
Click here to view the workflow status.

Number of reminders

The number of reminders to be sent

Time between reminders

Time calculation

Specifies whether or not hours outside the work week should be included when counting down to send a reminder.

During business days only

The During business days only option will specify that weekends or holidays are not included in the countdown.

During business hours only

The During business hours only option specifies that only business hours are used in the count down.

Escalation Notification Tab

When a task is assigned but is not completed Escalation rules can be defined to deal with un-completed tasks.

Configure Action - Assign to-do task

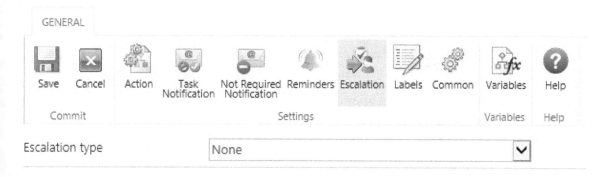

Escalation options are

- Delegate Task
- Complete Task

- Complete Workflow Task

This workflow action will complete any outstanding workflow tasks. It will process enough individual tasks to achieve the selected outcome.

Configure Action - Complete workflow task

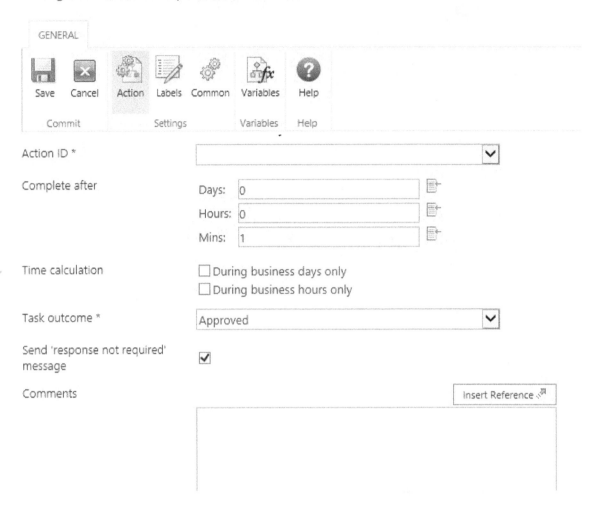

Action ID

Select a workflow variable of type Action ID which has been set to store a task action ID.

Complete after

How long should the workflow wait until it completes the task?

During business days only

The During business days only option will specify that weekends or holidays are not included in the countdown.

During business hours only

The During business hours only option specifies that only business hours are used in the count down.

Task Outcome

- Approved
- Rejected
- Continue

- Create Appointment

Use this workflow action to create a Microsoft Exchange calendar appointment for a specified user's mailbox. The appointment will be created in the specified user's mailbox, a meeting request will not be sent.

Configure Action - Create appointment

GENERAL

| Save | Cancel | Action | Attendees | Recurrence | Labels | Common | Variables | Help |

Commit · Settings · Variables · Help

Microsoft Exchange connection details

URL * `https://[Exchange Server]/ews/exchange.asmx`

Username *

Password

Editor mode *   ● Appointment ○ Advanced

Appointment details

For *

Start date * `2015-03-29T21:30:00`

End date * `2015-03-29T22:00:00`

Subject

Location

Body   Insert Reference

Importance Normal

Category

Reminder (minutes)

Private ☐

Microsoft Exchange connection details

URL - Microsoft Exchange Server URL

Username and Password for an account that has permissions to create appointments in the user mailbox in the **For** box

Editor Mode

- Appointment
- Advanced

For

The user mailbox to create the appointment in.

Start Date

The start date of the new appointment

End Date

The end date of the new appointment

Subject

A short subject about the new appointment

Location

The location of the new appointment

Body

More details about the new appointment

Importance

- High
- Normal
- Low

Reminder

The number of minutes prior to the Start Date to send a reminder

Private

Yes/No

Attendees Tab

This section allows the addition of additional meeting attendees. These users will receive meeting requests.

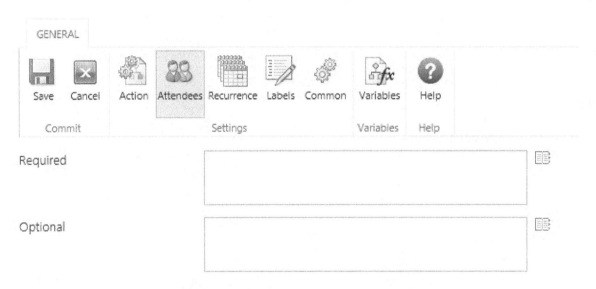

Recurrence Tab

This section specifies the recurrence pattern.

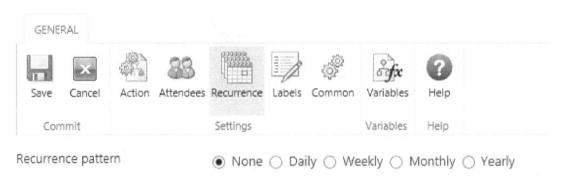

- Create Task

This workflow action creates new Microsoft Exchange.

Configure Action - Create task

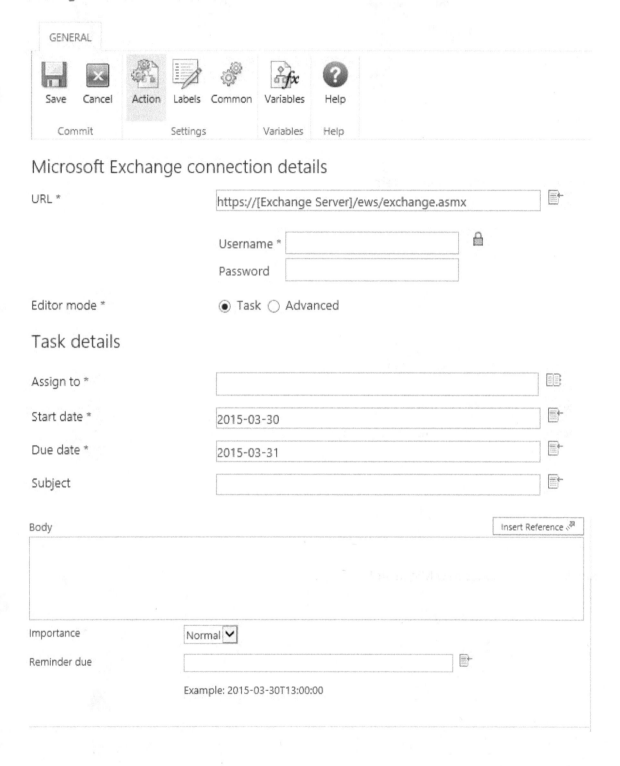

Microsoft Exchange connection details

URL - Microsoft Exchange Server URL

Username and Password for an account that has permissions to create appointments in the user mailbox in the **For** box

Editor Mode

- Appointment
- Advanced

Assign To

The users or groups who will be assigned the task. A task can be assigned to a single user or multiple users. If a task is assigned to multiple users explicitly (by listing each user) each user will have a task assigned to them individually. If a task is assigned only to a group one task will be assigned to that group. Any member of the group will be able to complete the task.

Start Date

The start date of the new appointment

Due Date

The due date of the new appointment

Subject

A short subject about the new appointment

Body

More details about the new appointment

Importance

- High
- Normal
- Low

Reminder

The number of minutes prior to send a reminder

- Delegate Workflow Task

This action will delegate outstanding workflow tasks to a specific user.

Configure Action - Delegate workflow task

GENERAL

Save   Cancel   Action   Labels   Common   Variables   Help

Commit   Settings   Variables   Help

Action ID *	[ ] ▼

Delegate after	Days:	0	
	Hours:	0	
	Mins:	0	

| Time calculation | ☐ During business days only |
| | ☐ During business hours only |

| Delegate to * | [   ] |

| Comments | Insert Reference |
| | [   ] |

| Apply to | ◉ All pending tasks |
| | ○ First pending task (other pending tasks will be not required) |

Action ID

Select a workflow variable of type Action ID which has been set to store a task action ID.

Delegate after

How long should the workflow wait until it delegates the task?

During business days only

The During business days only option will specify that weekends or holidays are not included in the countdown.

During business hours only

The During business hours only option specifies that only business hours are used in the count down.

Delegate To

The new assignee

Apply To

All pending tasks

First pending task

- Get Meeting Suggestions

This workflow action will retrieve a series of meeting time suggestions based on a specified criteria

Configure Action - Get meeting suggestions

GENERAL

Save	Cancel	Action	Labels	Common	Variables	Help

| Commit | | Settings | | Variables | Help |

Microsoft Exchange connection details

URL *   https://[Exchange Server]/ews/exchange.asmx

Username

Password

Meeting suggestion properties

Attendees *

Start after *   2015-03-30

End by *   2015-04-01

Meeting duration (minutes) *   30

Store result in *

⊟ Advanced

Maximum results per day *   16

Maximum non-business-hours results *   2

Define "Good" threshold for attendance *   75

Value must be between 51 and 99.

Minimum suggestion quality *   ○ Excellent ◉ Good ○ Fair ○ Poor

Result format   ◉ Text ○ XML

Microsoft Exchange connection details

URL - Microsoft Exchange Server URL

Username and Password for an account that has permissions to create appointments in the user mailbox in the **For** box

Attendees

The user mailboxes of the users who will be invited to the new meeting

Start After

The first possible start date of the new appointment

End By

The last possible end date of the new appointment

Store Result In

The workflow variable to store the results of the meeting suggestions in

Maximum Results per Day

The maximum number of meeting suggestions returned per day.

Maximum Non Business Hours Results per Day

The maximum number of meeting suggestions returned per day during non-business hours.

Define "Good" threshold for attendance

The percentage of attendees that must be able to attend a meeting suggestion for the suggestion to be given a "Good quality" status

Minimum suggestion quality

Excellent

Good

Fair

Poor

- Request Approval

This action allows the request of one or more users to process an approval as part of the workflow.

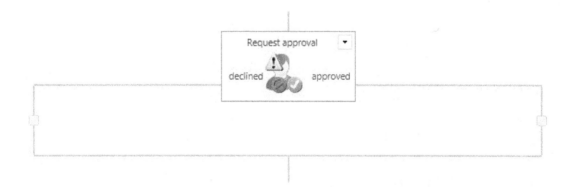

Configure Action - Request approval

GENERAL

Save	Cancel	Action	Task Notification	Not Required Notification	Edit Task Form ▾	Labels	Common	Variables	Help
Commit				Settings				Variables	Help

Approvers *

☐ Create individual tasks for all group members

Allow delegation ☐

Allow LazyApproval ☐ (only applicable with email delivery)

Task description

Insert Reference

Approval options

◉ All must approve   ○ First response applies

○ Only one approval is required   ○ Vote

Task name		
Task content type	Nintex Workflow Task	⌄
Priority	(2) Normal	
Due Date	Value ⌄	📅
Form type	Default	⌄
Store action ID in		⌄
Store task IDs in		⌄

☐ Item permissions

Set user permissions to	Unchanged ⌄
When task is complete, set user permissions to	Unchanged ⌄

Approvers

The users or groups who will be the approvers for the task. A task can a single approver or multiple approvers. If a task has multiple approvers explicitly (by listing each user) each user will have an approval task assigned to them individually. If an approval task is assigned only to a group one task will be assigned to that group. Any member of the group will be able to complete the approval task.

If the Create individual task for group members box is selected an individual task will be created and assigned to each member of the group.

Allow Delegation

Yes/No - Choose whether the assignee can delegate the task (or assign the task) to another person or group.

Allow LazyApproval

Yes/No - Choose whether the LazyApproval will be available to assignees.

The LazyApproval option allows assignees to complete their assigned task (either approving or rejecting) simply by replying to a Nintex generated email or OCS / Lync message.

The LazyApproval is only available when both incoming and outgoing email are configured within the SharePoint farm.

The LazyApproval is only available for on-premises SharePoint implementations, it is not available for Nintex Workflow for Office 365 (SharePoint Online).

The email response should be a single word (of a set of mapped words). All responses must map to either Approve or Deny. The table below shows the default Lazy Approval phrases and the outcome they map to:

Phrase	Outcome
approve	Approve
approved	Approve
decline	Deny
declined	Deny
no	Deny
ok	Approve
reject	Deny
rejected	Deny
yes	Approve

Task Description

Provide a longer description of the task being assigned.

Approval Options

The **Outcomes** define all the possible responses to the task. By default there are two possible outcomes:

- All Must Approve
- Only One Approval is Required
- First Response Applies
- Vote

Task Name

The title of the task. This title appears in the Workflow Task list for the task created.

Task Content Type

The content type of the task item created in the Workflow Task list

Priority

Select the Priority of the task created in the Workflow Task list

Due Date

The Task due date

Form Type

- Default
- Nintex

263

- InfoPath

Item Permissions

Allows you to set the user permission on the new task item, or leave them unchanged.

When task is complete, set user permissions to

Allows you to set the user permission on the new task item after the task has been completed, or leave them unchanged.

This can often be used when you want to make something read only after it has been completed.

Task Notification Tab

When a task is assigned to a user an email notification is sent to the assigned users. The Notification tab contains properties defining the notification email.

The email message can be modified, but the default is:

Configure Action - Request approval

GENERAL

Save	Cancel	Action	Task Notification	Not Required Notification	Edit Task Form ▾	Labels	Common	Variables	Help
Commit				Settings				Variables	Help

Edit settings for   All Approvers ☑

Allow delegation   ☐

Allow LazyApproval   ☐ (only applicable with email delivery)

Delivery type   ◉ Email ○ User preference ○ None

CC   [_____] ▤

BCC   [_____] ▤

From   [_____] ▤

Importance   Normal ☑

Subject   [Approval Required_____] ▤

Attachments   ☐ Attach file from workflow

     ✛ Add attachment

Edit settings for

Allows you to define specific edit settings for a specific assignee (assuming the task is assigned to more than one assignee)

Allow Delegation

Yes/No - Choose whether the assignee can delegate the task (or assign the task) to another person or group.

Allow LazyApproval

Yes/No - Choose whether the LazyApproval will be available to assignees.

Delivery Type

- None
- Email
- SMS / OCS/ Lync

The notification will automatically go to the assignees. You can also select CC and BCC recipients of the notification.

Not Required Notification Tab

When a task is assigned to multiple users and is completed before all users respond, those assignees who have not yet responded will receive an email notifying them that they do not need to do anything. The Notification not Required tab contains properties defining the notification email.

The email message can be modified, but the default is:

Configure Action - Request approval

GENERALES

Save	Cancel	Action	Task Notification	Not Required Notification	Edit Task Form	Labels	Common	Variables	Help
Commit				Settings				Variables	Help

Edit settings for   All Approvers ∨

Delivery type   ● Email ○ User preference ○ None

CC   [   ]

BCC   [   ]

From   [   ]

Importance   Normal ∨

Subject   Approval No Longer Required

Attachments   ☐ Attach file from workflow

         ⊕ Add attachment

Rich Text ∨   [Insert Reference ↗]

A task has been assigned to you regarding this item:

Context Item Display Name

Click here to respond to the task.
Click here to view the workflow status.

Edit settings for

Allows you to define specific edit settings for a specific assignee (assuming the task is assigned to more than one assignee)

Delivery Type

- None
- Email
- SMS / OCS/ Lync

The notification will automatically go to the assignees. You can also select CC and BCC recipients of the notification.

- Request Data

This workflow action assigns a task to a specified user. The action defines one or more values that the assignee must enter to complete the task. The Request Data action creates a new content type, with each requested value being added as a column to the content type.

Configure Action - Request data

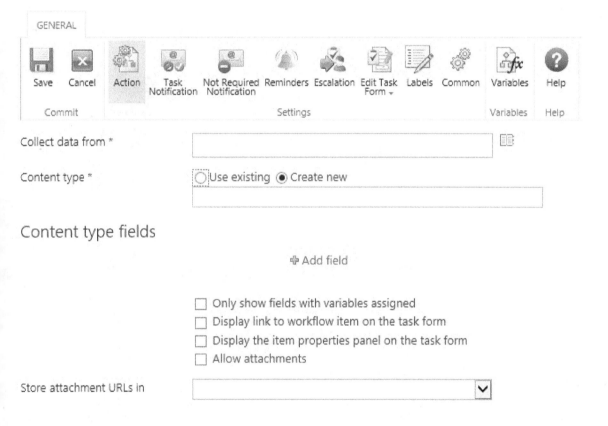

Content type fields

+ Add field

☐ Only show fields with variables assigned
☐ Display link to workflow item on the task form
☐ Display the item properties panel on the task form
☐ Allow attachments

Store attachment URLs in

Task description   Insert Reference

> Please enter the following information.

Allow delegation   ☐

Enable responses by email using LazyApproval   ☐ only applicable with email delivery

Task name

Priority   (2) Normal

Due Date   Value ▼

Store action ID in   ▼

Store task ID in   ▼

Form type   Default ▼

⊟ Item permissions

Set user permissions to   Unchanged ▼

When task is complete, set user permissions to   Unchanged ▼

Collect Data From

The users or groups who will be requested to input the requested values. A request data task can be assigned to a single user or multiple users. If a task is assigned to multiple users explicitly (by listing each user) each user will have a task assigned to them individually. If a task is assigned only to a group one task will be assigned to that group. Any member of the group will be able to complete the task.

270

Content Type

    New

    Existing

Content Type Fields

Add additional fields to the content type. These fields are the values you are requesting from the task assignees.

Name	
Type	Single line of text ▾
Default value	
Required	☐

                                                     OK   Cancel

Store Attachment URLs in

A workflow variable that will store the url to any item attachments

Task Description

Provide a longer description of the task being assigned.

Allow Delegation

Yes/No - Choose whether the assignee can delegate the task (or assign the task) to another person or group.

Allow LazyApproval

Yes/No - Choose whether the LazyApproval will be available to assignees.

The LazyApproval option allows assignees to complete their assigned task (either approving or rejecting) simply by replying to a Nintex generated email or OCS / Lync message.

The LazyApproval is only available when both incoming and outgoing email are configured within the SharePoint farm.

The LazyApproval is only available for on-premises SharePoint implementations, it is not available for Nintex Workflow for Office 365 (SharePoint Online).

Task Name

The title of the task. This title appears in the Workflow Task list for the task created.

Priority

Select the Priority of the task created in the Workflow Task list

Due Date

The Task due date

Form Type

- Default
- Nintex
- InfoPath

Item Permissions

Allows you to set the user permission on the new task item, or leave them unchanged.

When task is complete, set user permissions to

Allows you to set the user permission on the new task item after the task has been completed, or leave them unchanged.

This can often be used when you want to make something read only after it has been completed.

Task Notification Tab

When a task is assigned to a user an email notification is sent to the assigned users. The Notification tab contains properties defining the notification email.

The email message can be modified, but the default is:

Configure Action - Request data

GENERAL

| Save | Cancel | Action | Task Notification | Not Required Notification | Reminders | Escalation | Edit Task Form | Labels | Common | Variables | Help |

| Commit | | | | | | Settings | | | | Variables | Help |

Delivery type   ● Email   ○ User preference   ○ None

CC   [   ]

BCC   [   ]

From   [   ]

Importance   [Normal ▼]

Subject   [Input required]

Attachments   ☐ Attach file from workflow

＋ Add attachment

Delivery Type

- None
- Email
- SMS / OCS/ Lync

The notification will automatically go to the assignees. You can also select CC and BCC recipients of the notification.

Not Required Notification Tab

When a task is assigned to multiple users and is completed before all users respond, those assignees who have not yet responded will receive an email notifying them that they do not need to do anything. The Notification not Required tab contains properties defining the notification email.

The email message can be modified, but the default is:

Configure Action - Request data

GENERAL

| Save | Cancel | Action | Task Notification | Not Required Notification | Reminders | Escalation | Edit Task Form | Labels | Common | Variables | Help |

| Commit | | | | Settings | | | | | | Variables | Help |

Delivery type	● Email ○ User preference ○ None
CC	
BCC	
From	
Importance	Normal ⌄
Subject	Input no longer required
Attachments	☐ Attach file from workflow
	⊕ Add attachment

Rich Text ⌄   Insert Reference ⤢

A task has been assigned to you regarding this item:

Context Item Display Name

Click here to respond to the task.
Click here to view the workflow status.

Delivery Type

- None
- Email
- SMS / OCS/ Lync

The notification will automatically go to the assignees. You can also select CC and BCC recipients of the notification.

Reminders Notification Tab

When a task is assigned you can define reminders, which are additional notifications sent to assignees who have not completed the task within a defined time period.

Configure Action - Request data

GENERAL

Save	Cancel	Action	Task Notification	Not Required Notification	Reminders	Escalation	Edit Task Form ▾	Labels	Common	Variables	Help
Commit						Settings				Variables	Help

Number of reminders   [0]

Time between reminders
  Days: [0]
  Hours: [0]
  Mins: [0]

Time calculation   ☐ During business days only
                     ☐ During business hours only

CC   [   ]

BCC   [   ]

From   [   ]

Importance   [Normal ▾]

Subject [   ]

Attach file   ☐

[Rich Text ▾]   [Insert Reference ↗]

A task has been assigned to you regarding this item:

Context Item Display Name

Click here to respond to the task.
Click here to view the workflow status.

Number of reminders

The number of reminders to be sent

Time between reminders

Time calculation

Specifies whether or not hours outside the work week should be included when counting down to send a reminder.

During business days only

The During business days only option will specify that weekends or holidays are not included in the countdown.

During business hours only

The During business hours only option specifies that only business hours are used in the count down.

Escalation Notification Tab

When a task is assigned but is not completed Escalation rules can be defined to deal with un-completed tasks.

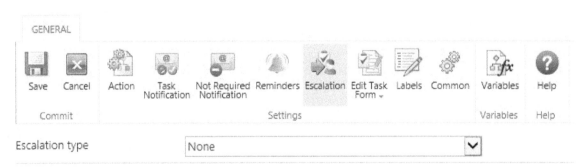

Escalation options are

> Delegate Task

> Complete Task

- Request Review

This action is used to assign a task and send a notification to one or more users to review an item as part of the workflow. For more details on the review process please refer to Approving, Rejecting and Reviewing Items.

Configure Action - Request review

GENERAL

Save	Cancel	Action	Task Notification	Not Required Notification	Edit Task Form ▾	Labels	Common	Variables	Help

Commit   Settings   Variables   Help

Reviewers *

☐ Create individual tasks for all group members

Allow delegation   ☐

Allow LazyApproval   ☐ (only applicable with email delivery)

Task description   Insert Reference ⬈

Review options   ◉ All must review
                 ○ First response applies

Task name

Task content type	Nintex Workflow Task ▼
Priority	(2) Normal
Due Date	Value ▼
Form type	Default ▼
Store action ID in	▼
Store task IDs in	▼

☐ Item permissions

Set user permissions to	Unchanged ▼
When task is complete, set user permissions to	Unchanged ▼

Reviewers

The users or groups who will be requested to review the item A request review task can be assigned to a single user or multiple users. If a task is assigned to multiple users explicitly (by listing each user) each user will have a task assigned to them individually. If a task is assigned only to a group one task will be assigned to that group. Any member of the group will be able to complete the task.

Allow Delegation

Yes/No - Choose whether the assignee can delegate the task (or assign the task) to another person or group.

Allow LazyApproval

Yes/No - Choose whether the LazyApproval will be available to assignees.

The LazyApproval option allows assignees to complete their assigned task (either approving or rejecting) simply by replying to a Nintex generated email or OCS / Lync message.

The LazyApproval is only available when both incoming and outgoing email are configured within the SharePoint farm.

The LazyApproval is only available for on-premises SharePoint implementations, it is not available for Nintex Workflow for Office 365 (SharePoint Online).

Task Description

Provide a longer description of the task being assigned.

Review Options

>   All Must Review

>   First Response Applies

Task Name

The title of the task. This title appears in the Workflow Task list for the task created.

Priority

Select the Priority of the task created in the Workflow Task list

Due Date

The Task due date

Form Type

- Default
- Nintex
- InfoPath

Item Permissions

Allows you to set the user permission on the new task item, or leave them unchanged.

When task is complete, set user permissions to

Allows you to set the user permission on the new task item after the task has been completed, or leave them unchanged.

This can often be used when you want to make something read only after it has been completed.

Task Notification Tab

When a task is assigned to a user an email notification is sent to the assigned users. The Notification tab contains properties defining the notification email.

The email message can be modified, but the default is:

Configure Action - Request review

GENERAL

| Save | Cancel | Action | Task Notification | Not Required Notification | Edit Task Form | Labels | Common | Variables | Help |

| Commit | | Settings | | Variables | Help |

Edit settings for   All Reviewers ☑

Allow delegation   ☐

Allow LazyApproval   ☐ (only applicable with email delivery)

Delivery type   ◉ Email ○ User preference ○ None

CC   [_____]

BCC   [_____]

From   [_____]

Importance   Normal ☑

Subject   Review Required

Attachments   ☐ Attach file from workflow

✚ Add attachment

Edit settings for

Allows you to define specific edit settings for a specific reviewer (assuming the task is assigned to more than one assignee)

Allow Delegation

Yes/No - Choose whether the assignee can delegate the task (or assign the task) to another person or group.

284

Allow LazyApproval

Yes/No - Choose whether the LazyApproval will be available to assignees.

Delivery Type

- None
- Email
- SMS / OCS/ Lync

The notification will automatically go to the assignees. You can also select CC and BCC recipients of the notification.

Not Required Notification Tab

When a task is assigned to multiple users and is completed before all users respond, those assignees who have not yet responded will receive an email notifying them that they do not need to do anything. The Notification not Required tab contains properties defining the notification email.

The email message can be modified, but the default is:

Configure Action - Request review

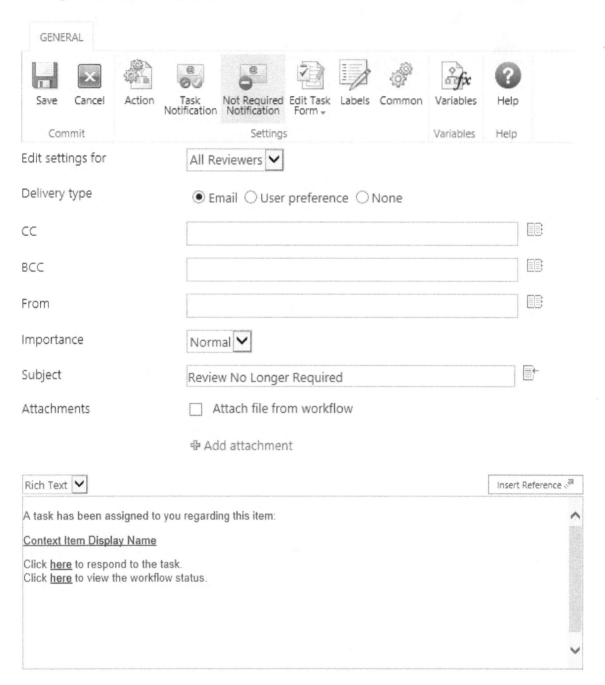

Edit settings for

Allows you to define specific edit settings for a specific reviewer (assuming the task is assigned to more than one assignee)

Delivery Type

- None
- Email
- SMS / OCS/ Lync

The notification will automatically go to the assignees. You can also select CC and BCC recipients of the notification.

- Send Notification

Use the Send Notification workflow action to define and send an email message to another user or users

Configure Action - Send notification

GENERAL

| Save | Cancel | Action | Labels | Common | Variables | Help |

Commit | Settings | Variables | Help

To *

☑ Send individually addressed notifications

CC

BCC

From

Importance   Normal ▼

Subject *

Attachments   ☐ Attach file from workflow

✚ Add attachment

Rich Text ▼   Insert Reference ⤢

Delivery type   ⦿ Email ◯ User preference

To

The email address the notification is being sent to

From

The email address the notification is from

Importance

High

Normal

Low

Subject

The Subject of the Email

- Task Reminder

Use the Task Reminder workflow action to email notifications to the approvers or reviewers of an outstanding task.

Configure Action - Task reminder

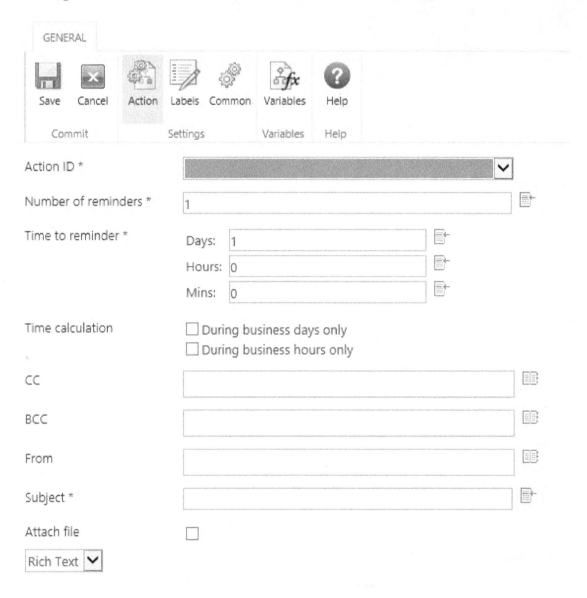

Action ID

Select a workflow variable of type Action ID which has been set to store a task action ID.

Number of Reminders

How many reminders should Nintex send?

During business days only

The During business days only option will specify that weekends or holidays are not included in the countdown.

During business hours only

The During business hours only option specifies that only business hours are used in the count down.

Demo 6 - Assign a Task with Lazy Approval in Office 365
will work with on-premises SharePoint but is called the 'Assign to do Task'

The SharePoint Online version of Nintex Workflow does not have the Flexi Task action, one option is to use the **Assign a Task** action instead of a Flexi Task.

- Create a new task list to use for Workflow Tasks

- On the **Gear** icon click **Add an App**

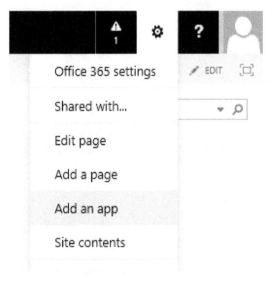

- Select **Tasks** on the **Your Apps** page

- Name the new task list **YourName_WF_Tasks**

- Now create an out of the box **Document Library**

- On the **Gear** icon click **Add an App**

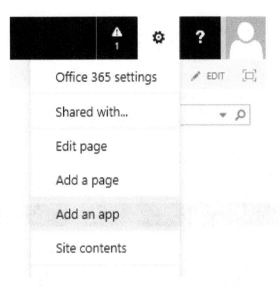

- Select **Document Library** on the **Your Apps** page

Document Library
Popular built-in app
App Details

Custom List
Popular built-in app
App Details

Tasks
Popular built-in app
App Details

Site Mailbox
Popular built-in app
App Details

- Name the Document Library **YourName_WF_Documents**

Adding Document Library   ✕

Pick a name
You can add this app multiple times to your site. Give it a unique name.

Name:

MikeM_WF_Documents

Advanced Options

[Create]   [Cancel]

- Click on the new library name to navigate to the library
- Click **Library Settings** on the **Library tab** of the ribbon

- On the **Library Settings** page click **Versioning Settings**

MikeM_WF_Documents › Settings

List Information

Name: MikeM_WF_Documents

Web Address: https://xspects.sharepoint.com/Team/Nintex/MikeM_WF_Documents/Forms/AllItems.aspx

Description:

General Settings

- List name, description and navigation
- Versioning settings
- Advanced settings
- Validation settings
- Column default value settings
- Audience targeting settings
- Rating settings
- Form settings
- Catalog Settings

Permissions and Management

- Delete this document library
- Save document library as template
- Permissions for this document library
- Manage files which have no checked in version
- Workflow Settings
- Generate file plan report
- Enterprise Metadata and Keywords Settings
- Information management policy settings

- On the **Versioning Settings** page select **Yes** to **Require content approval for submitted items** and scroll down and click **OK**

Require content approval for submitted items?
◉ Yes   ○ No

- Click **Nintex Workflow** on the **Library** tab of the ribbon

- Click **Settings** on the **Workflow Designer** ribbon

- On the **Workflow Settings** page enter *Task Action Approval* as the Name. Select the task list you just created as the **Task List**, and select **Start when items are created** and click **Save**

- Drag the **Assign a Task** action onto the design canvas (the **Assign a task** action is in the **User Interaction** section)

- Click the down arrow on the action and click **Configure**

- On the **Configure** page enter your own email address in the Participants field. Enter *A document needs to be reviewed* as the **Task Title**. Select tomorrows date as the **Due Date**. Scroll down and observe the **Task Creation Email Options** and the **Task Overdue Reminder Email Options**, and the **Task Cancellation Email Options**.

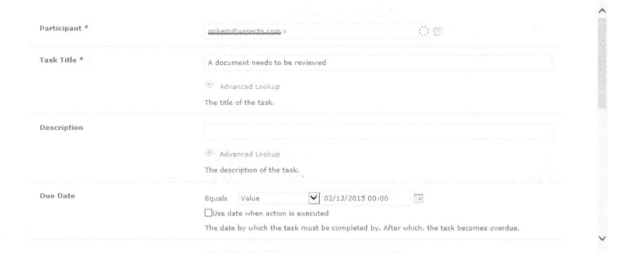

- Just like the **Flexi Task** the standard task sends an email

 Reply Reply All Forward

Sun 2/8/2015 9:29 PM

Nintex <no-reply@sharepointonline.com>

Task Assigned - A document needs to be reviewed

To   Michael McManus

You have a new task.

A document needs to be reviewed

ASSIGNED TO   Michael McManus

DUE DATE   2/13/2015 12:00:00 AM

DESCRIPTION

RELATED ITEM   Sample 1

- Scroll down and select the **Allow Lazy Approval** option. Just as we saw in the **Flexi Task** action with on-premises SharePoint the **Assign a Task** action in Office 365 allows Assignees to respond to an assigned task via email.

- **Save** the Task action

- Drag the **Office 365 Set Approval Status** action into the **Approved** path

- Click the action dropdown arrow and click **Configure**

- On the **Configure** page click **Advanced Lookup** for the **Destination Site URL.** Select **Workflow Context** and **Current site URL** and click **Insert**

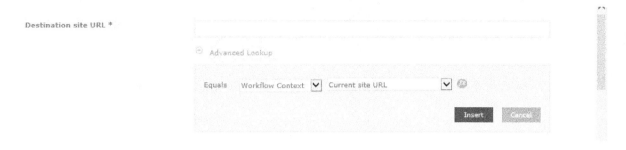

- On the **Configure** page click **Advanced Lookup** for the **List Name** select **Workflow Context, List Name** and click **Insert**

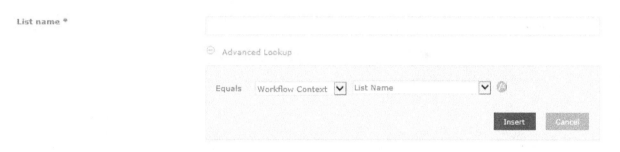

- On the **Configure** page click **Advanced Lookup** for the **SharePoint Online URL** select **Workflow Context, Current Site URL** and click **Insert**

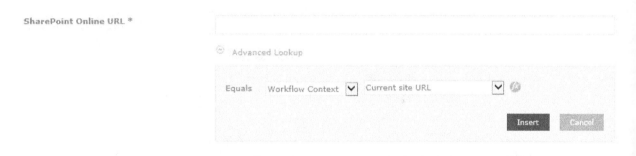

- On the **Configure** page for the **Username** type in your Office 365 email address and click **Insert**

- On the **Configure** page for the **Password** type in your Office 365 Password and click **Insert**

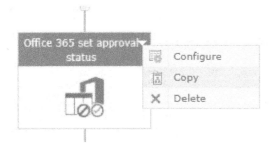

- On the **Configure** page for the **Approval Status** select **Approved** and **click Insert**

- Click **Save**

- Click the dropdown arrow on the action and click **Copy**

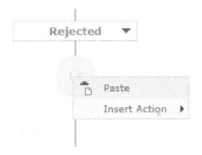

- Place your cursor on the bubble in the **Rejected** path, right click and click **Paste**

- Click the action dropdown arrow and click **Configure**

- Leave all the values as they are except the **Approval Status** which should be changed to **Rejected**

- **Save** and **Publish** the Workflow

Collections and Looping

Collections are groups of things. It really is that simple. Why are collections important in Nintex Workflows?

Collections allow us to 'loop through' multiple similar items and perform the same operations on all of those similar items.

Pretend we have ten birdhouses. Each birdhouse needs to be painted - red roof, yellow sides, blue base.

Luckily we have 3 helpers. Jon will paint all the roofs red; Sally will paint all the sides yellow; I will paint all the bases blue. We decide to simply work like an assembly line, in sequence. I take one birdhouse off the pile and paint the base blue; I pass it to Sally who paints the sides yellow; Sally passes it to Jon who paints the roof red. We then repeat the exact same process for each of the nine remaining birdhouses.

In this example the group of 10 birdhouses is the Collection. The three helpers (Jon, Sally and I) are three workflow actions. The process of us repeating our individual tasks in sequence on the 10 birdhouses is the loop.

Think of this situation. We want our users to be able to request a new web site in our SharePoint intranet. We do not want to give all of these users the necessary permissions to create new web sites themselves. Ideally users should be able to request a new site, the request would then be either approved or rejected by their supervisor and by an IT site administrator. Requests that are fully approved would then be created automatically in a nightly batch.

We can accomplish the above scenario using a site workflow, a collection variable, a 'For Each' workflow action and a new SharePoint list. In Demo 7 we will build this workflow, but for now let's think about it conceptually.

A user request is simple, the user inputs the title and url of their requested site.

The requesting employee's manager is assigned an approval task; if the manager approves the request another approval task is assigned to the IT supervisor.

If the IT supervisor approves the site will be created during the next nightly batch.

A site workflow is created and scheduled to run every night at 10:00 PM. The site workflow filters for only items that have been approved by both the manager and the IT supervisor such as examples 2 and 3 below:

Site Title	Site Url	Manager Approval	IT Approval
Example 1	Ex1	Yes	No
Example 2	Ex2	Yes	Yes
Example 3	Ex3	Yes	Yes

When the workflow executes a list query filtered as above two items are returned. These two items are the collection!

Our collection variable now 'contains' two list items, Example 2 and Example 3.

Using the For Each workflow action we can define a group of actions that will be repeated for each item in the collection, in this case we create a new site using the Site Title and Site Url values for each item in the collection (the two items that met our filter criteria).

Collections

In this table each row is an item in the collection represented by the entire table.

Site Title	Site Url	Manager Approval	IT Approval
Example 1	Ex1	Yes	No
Example 2	Ex2	Yes	Yes
Example 3	Ex3	Yes	Yes

Collections are implemented as workflow variables which are populated by a workflow action that returns multiple items, such as one of the query workflow flow actions.

Loops

The primary workflow action used to implement looping is the For Each workflow action. The For Each workflow action requires two workflow variables - one representing the target collection (the collection of items to loop through) and one which will represent each individual item, each time the workflow action loops.

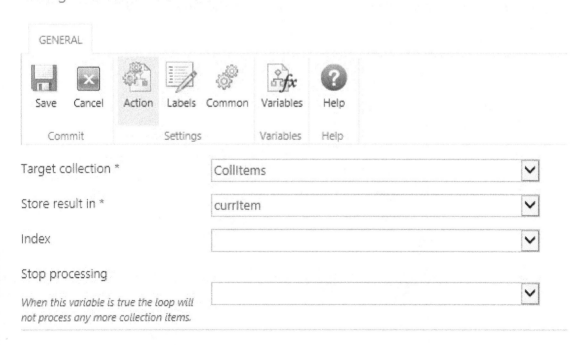

Safe looping and delays between iterations

A loop that is configured to run for many iterations without a pause can cause the workflow to use excessive system resources. As a precaution, a hidden delay is automatically added at the end of each iteration if the child actions are not guaranteed to cause the workflow to stop and wait. This can cause a 2 - 7 minute pause between each run of the loop. This option is called 'Safe Looping'. Administrators can disable Safe Looping from the Global Settings in Central Administration. The hidden delay is added when the workflow is published, so if the Safe Looping option is changed it will only affect any newly published workflows. However, any existing workflows will need to be republished to see the change in the behavior.

Demo 7 - Collections and Looping

In this demo we will implement a custom list, two list workflows and a site workflow to solve the Use Case discussed above:

We want our users to be able to request a new web site in our SharePoint intranet. We do not want to give all of these users the necessary permissions to create new web sites themselves. Ideally users should be able to request a new site, the request would then be either approved or rejected by their supervisor and by an IT site administrator. Requests that are fully approved would then be created automatically in a nightly batch.

We will fulfill the requirements of the above Use Case in four steps:

- Create a new SharePoint list which our users will enter items into to request a new site

Site Title	Site Url	Manager Approval	IT Approval
Example 1	Ex1	Yes	No
Example 2	Ex2	Yes	Yes
Example 3	Ex3	Yes	Yes

- Create an Approval Workflow on the New Site List to assign an approval request to the manager, and if approved by the manager request approval from the IT supervisor.
- Create an Approval Workflow on the New Site List to assign an approval request to the IT supervisor.
- Create and Schedule a Site Workflow to create sites based on items in the New Site List that have been approved by both the manager and the IT supervisor.

CREATE NEW SITE REQUEST LIST

- Click **Add an App** on the 'gear' dropdown menu

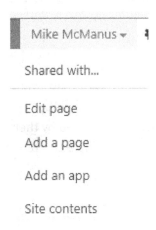

- On the **Site Contents** page click **Custom List** to create a new list using the Custom List template

Site Contents · Your Apps

Noteworthy

Document Library
Popular built-in app
App Details

Custom List
Popular built-in app
App Details

Tasks
Popular built-in app
App Details

- Enter '**New Sites**' as the name on the Adding Custom List page and click '**Create**'

Adding Custom List   ✕

Pick a name

You can add this app multiple times to your site. Give it a
unique name.

Name:

New Sites

Advanced Options   Create   Cancel

- On the **Site Contents** page click the ellipses in the upper right of the **New Sites** list panel and click '**Settings**' to open the list's settings page

- On the list settings page click '**Create Column**'

Columns

A column stores information about each item in th

Column (click to edit)

Title

Modified

Created

Created By

Modified By

- Create column

- Add from existing site columns

- Column ordering

- On the Create Column page enter '**SiteTitle**' as the column name and click **OK**

Settings ⸱ Create Column ⓘ

Name and Type

Type a name for this column, and select the type of information you want to store in the column.

Column name:

SiteTitle   ✕

The type of information in this column is:

- ⦿ Single line of text
- ○ Multiple lines of text
- ○ Choice (menu to choose from)
- ○ Number (1, 1.0, 100)

- On the list settings page click 'Create Column'
- On the Create Column page enter 'SiteURL' as the column name and click OK

Settings ⸱ Create Column ⓘ

Name and Type

Type a name for this column, and select the type of information you want to store in the column.

Column name:

SiteURL

The type of information in this column is:

- ⦿ Single line of text
- ○ Multiple lines of text
- ○ Choice (menu to choose from)

- On the list settings page click '**Create Column**'
- On the Create Column page enter '**ManagerApproval**' as the column name, Yes/No Checkbox as the column type, and click **OK**

- Ensure the default value is **No**

Name and Type

Type a name for this column, and select
the type of information you want to store
in the column.

Column name:

| ManagerApproval |

The type of information in this column is:

- ○ Single line of text
- ○ Multiple lines of text
- ○ Choice (menu to choose from)
- ○ Number (1, 1.0, 100)
- ○ Currency ($, ¥, €)
- ○ Date and Time
- ○ Lookup (information already on this site)
- ● Yes/No (check box)
- ○ Person or Group
- ○ Hyperlink or Picture
- ○ Calculated (calculation based on other columns)
- ○ Task Outcome
- ○ External Data
- ○ Managed Metadata

Additional Column Settings

Specify detailed options for the type of
information you selected.

Description:

Default value:

No ▼

- On the list settings page click **Create Column**
- On the Create Column page enter **ITApproval** as the column name, **Yes/No** Checkbox as the column type, and click **OK**
- Ensure the default value is **No**

Name and Type

Type a name for this column, and select the type of information you want to store in the column.

Column name:

ITApproval

The type of information in this column is:

○ Single line of text
○ Multiple lines of text
○ Choice (menu to choose from)
○ Number (1, 1.0, 100)
○ Currency ($, ¥, €)
○ Date and Time
○ Lookup (information already on this site)
◉ Yes/No (check box)
○ Person or Group
○ Hyperlink or Picture
○ Calculated (calculation based on other columns)
○ Task Outcome
○ External Data
○ Managed Metadata

Additional Column Settings

Specify detailed options for the type of information you selected.

Description:

Default value:

No ▾

CREATE NEW WORKFLOW TO REQUEST IT APPROVAL

- On the List ribbon of the **New Sites** list click **Create a Workflow in Nintex Workflow** on the **Workflow Settings** menu

- On the 'Select a Workflow Template' page select Blank and click Create

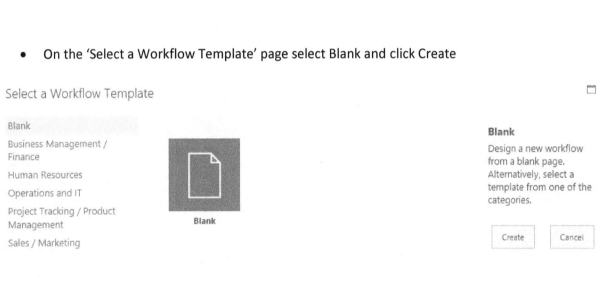

- Click **Workflow Settings** to open the workflow settings page

- On the Workflow Settings page enter **New Site IT Approval** as the workflow name and click **Save**

Workflow Settings

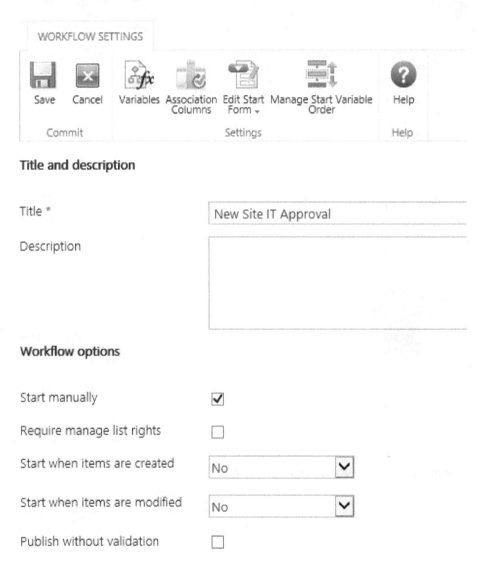

Title and description

Title *

New Site IT Approval

Description

Workflow options

Start manually   ☑

Require manage list rights   ☐

Start when items are created   No ▼

Start when items are modified   No ▼

Publish without validation   ☐

- On the design canvas drag an **Assign a Flexi** Task action under the green **Start** arrow

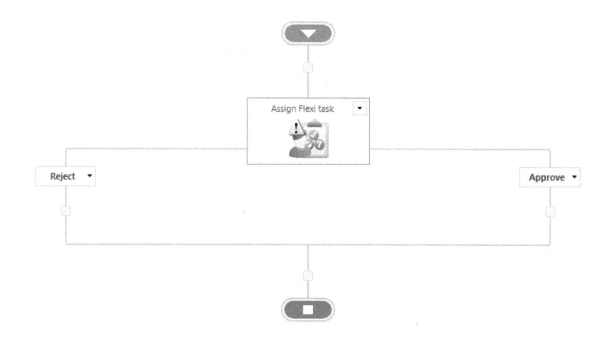

- Open the **Assign Flexi Task** configuration page
- Assign the task to yourself (we will pretend you are the IT supervisor)
- Save the action - leave the default values

Configure Action - Assign Flexi task

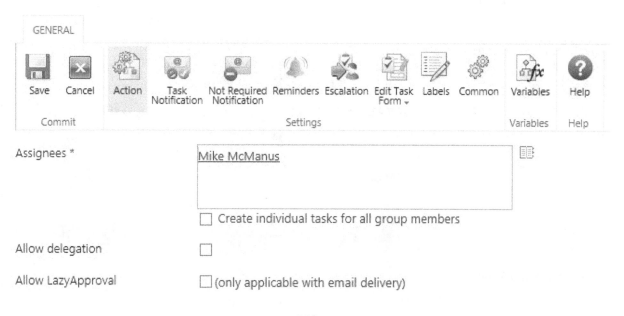

- Drag a **Set Field Value** workflow action into the **Approve** branch of the **Assign Flexi Task** action

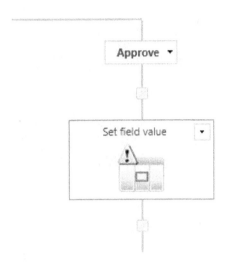

- Open the **Set Field Value** action configuration page
- Select the **ITApproval** field equal to **Yes** as below

Configure Action - Set field value

- Save and Publish the workflow

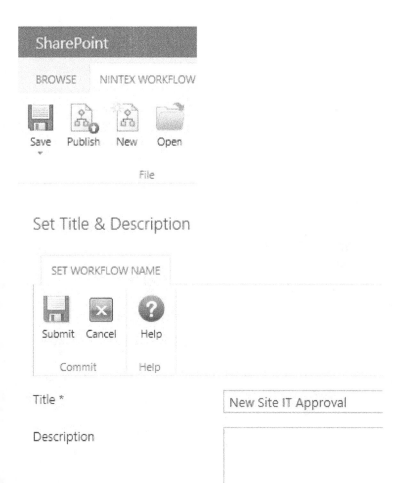

CREATE NEW WORKFLOW TO REQUEST MANAGER APPROVAL

- On the List ribbon of the New Sites list click 'Create a Workflow in Nintex Workflow' on the Workflow Settings menu

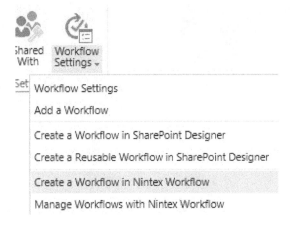

- On the 'Select a Workflow Template' page select Blank and click Create

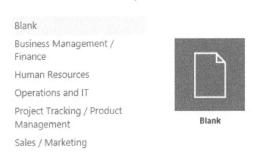

- Click 'Workflow Settings' to open the workflow settings page

- On the Workflow Settings page enter 'New Site Manager Approval' as the workflow name and click Save

Workflow Settings

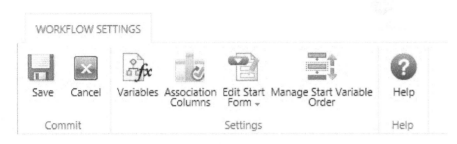

Title and description

Title *   New Site Manager Approval

Description

Workflow options

Start manually   ☑

Require manage list rights   ☐

Start when items are created | Yes |

Start when items are modified | No |

Publish without validation   ☐

- On the **Workflow settings** page click **Variables**

Workflow Variables

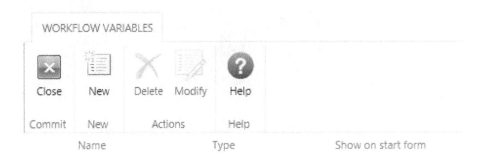

Name	Type	Show on start form

- On the Workflow Variables page click 'New'
- Enter **ManagerApproval** as the Name and choose Yes/No as the type

Create Workflow Variable

Name		ManagerApproval

Type

- ○ Single line of text   ○ Person or Group
- ○ Multiple lines of text   ○ Integer
- ○ Choice   ○ List Item ID
- ○ Number   ○ Action ID
- ○ Date and Time   ○ Collection
- ◉ Yes/No

Default value   No ▾

Show on start form   ☐

Workflow Variables

Name	Type	Show on start form
ManagerApproval	Yes/No	No

- On the design canvas drag an **Assign a Flexi Task** action under the green Start arrow

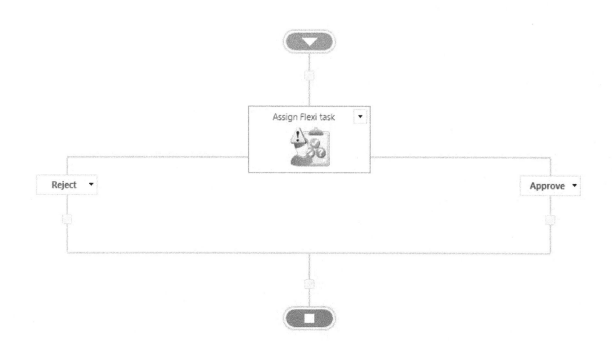

- Open the **Assign Flexi Task configuration** page
- Assign the task to the initiator's (requestor's)
- Click the People Picker to the right of the Assignees box

Configure Action - Assign Flexi task

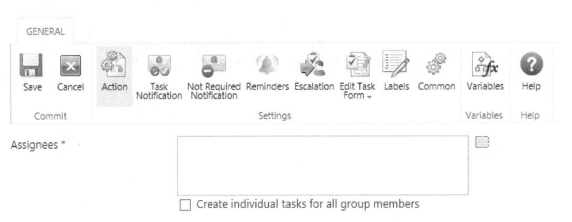

- On the Select People and Groups page choose the **Lookup** tab and select **Manager**
- Click **Add** and **OK**

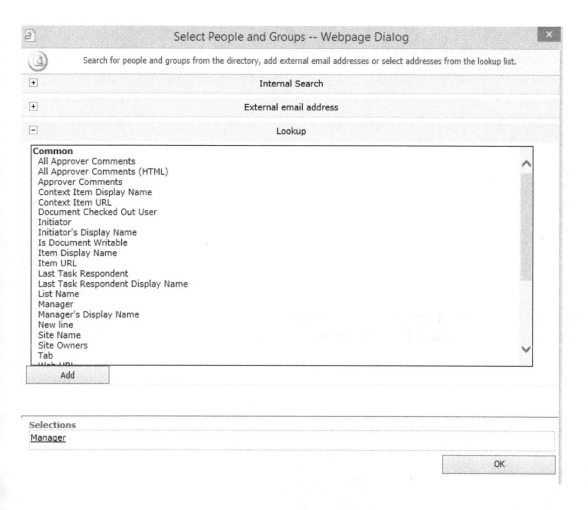

- Select to store the outcome achieved in the **ManagerApproval** workflow variable

- **Save** the action - leave the remaining default values

- Drag a **Set Field Value** workflow action into the **Approve** branch of the **Assign Flexi Task** action

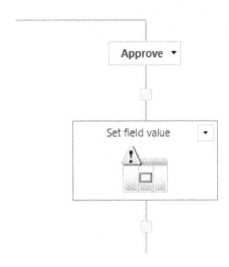

- Open the **Set Field Value** action configuration page
- Select the **ManagerApproval** field equal to **Yes** as below

Configure Action - Set field value

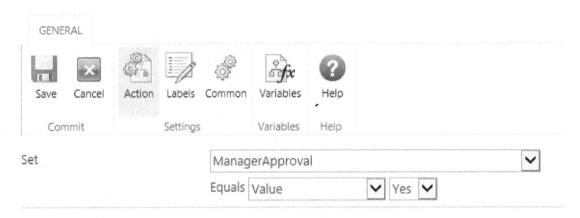

- Drag a **Start a Workflow** action under the **Set Field Value** action

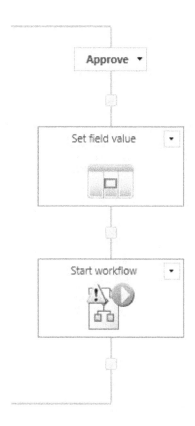

- Open the **Start Workflow** action **configuration** page
- Select the **New Site IT Approval** workflow as the workflow to start. This will start the IT supervisor approval workflow, but only after the manager approval has been completed and approved

Configure Action - Start workflow

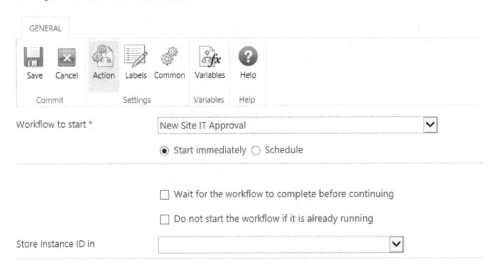

Workflow to start *   New Site IT Approval

⦿ Start immediately ◯ Schedule

☐ Wait for the workflow to complete before continuing

☐ Do not start the workflow if it is already running

Store instance ID in

- **Save** the **Start Workflow Action**

- **Save** and **Publish** the workflow

CREATE THE SITE WORKFLOW TO LOOP

- On the 'Gear' icon to the right of your name select Nintex Workflow 2013 >> Create Site Workflow

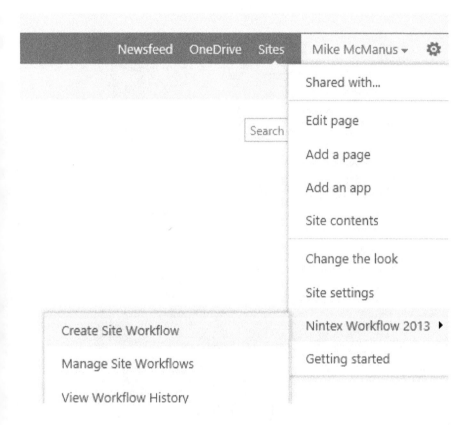

- On **Workflow Settings** page enter the name **Create New Sites**

Workflow Settings

WORKFLOW SETTINGS

Save	Cancel	Variables	Association Columns	Edit Start Form ▾	Manage Start Variable Order	Help
Commit				Settings		Help

Title and description

Title *   Create New Sites

Description

Workflow options

Start manually   ☑

Require manage web rights   ☐

- Click **Variables** on the ribbon
- On the **Create Workflow Variables** page click **New**
- Create a variable named '**CollItems**' of type '**Collection**'

Create Workflow Variable

WORKFLOW VARIABLES

Save	Cancel	Help
Commit		Help

Name

CollItems

Type

- ○ Single line of text   ○ Person or Group
- ○ Multiple lines of text ○ Integer
- ○ Choice   ○ List Item ID
- ○ Number   ○ Action ID
- ○ Date and Time   ● Collection
- ○ Yes/No

Show on start form   ☐

- **Save** the variable
- Click **New** to create a second variable
- On the **Create Workflow Variable** page enter 'currItem' as the name and select 'List Item ID' as the type. This variable will be used to keep track of where we are in the collection as we loop through all of the items.

Create Workflow Variable

WORKFLOW VARIABLES

Save	Cancel	Help
Commit		Help

Name   currItem

Type

○ Single line of text   ○ Person or Group
○ Multiple lines of text   ○ Integer
○ Choice   ◉ List Item ID
○ Number   ○ Action ID
○ Date and Time   ○ Collection
○ Yes/No

Show on start form   ☐

- **Save** the variable
- Click **New** to create a third variable
- On the Create Workflow Variable page enter '**SiteName**' as the name and select '**Single Line of Text**' as the type.

Create Workflow Variable

WORKFLOW VARIABLES		
Save	Cancel	Help
Commit		Help

Name

SiteName

Type

◉ Single line of text   ○ Person or Group

○ Multiple lines of text   ○ Integer

○ Choice   ○ List Item ID

○ Number   ○ Action ID

○ Date and Time   ○ Collection

○ Yes/No

Default value

Show on start form   ☐

- **Save** the variable
- Click '**New**' to create a fourth variable
- On the **Create Workflow Variable** page enter **SiteURL** as the name and select **Single Line of Text** as the type.

Create Workflow Variable

WORKFLOW VARIABLES

Save   Cancel   Help

Commit   Help

Name   SiteURL

Type   ● Single line of text   ○ Person or Group
                                ○ Multiple lines of text   ○ Integer
                                ○ Choice   ○ List Item ID
                                ○ Number   ○ Action ID
                                ○ Date and Time   ○ Collection
                                ○ Yes/No

Default value

Show on start form   ☐

- **Save** the variable
- Drag the **Query List** workflow action onto the design canvas under the green Start icon

- Open the '**Query List**' action **configuration** page
- Select the '**New Sites**' list

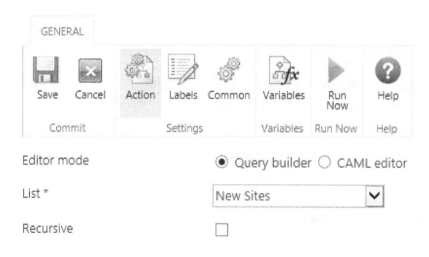

- Expand the **Filter** section and create two filters connected by an 'And' as below

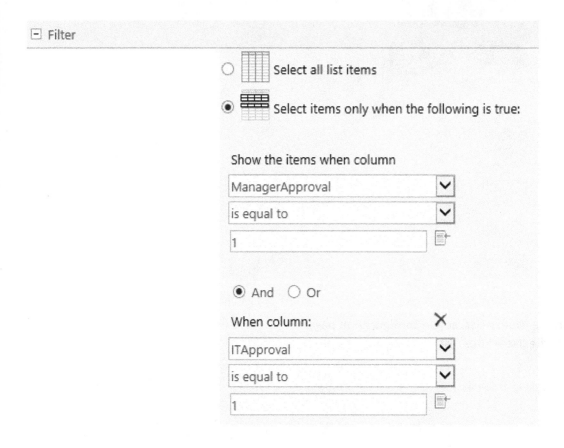

- Click 'Add' to the right of 'Field' and select ID to add the item ID field to the collection
- Choose to save the ID field in the 'CollItems' collection variable

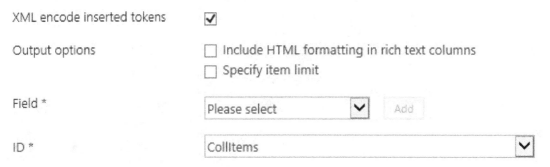

- Drag a 'For Each' workflow action under the Query List action

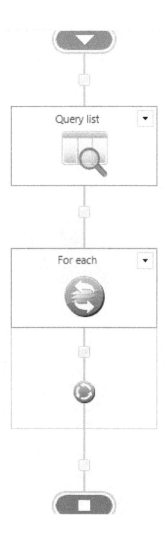

- Open the '**For Each**' action configuration page

Configure Action - For each

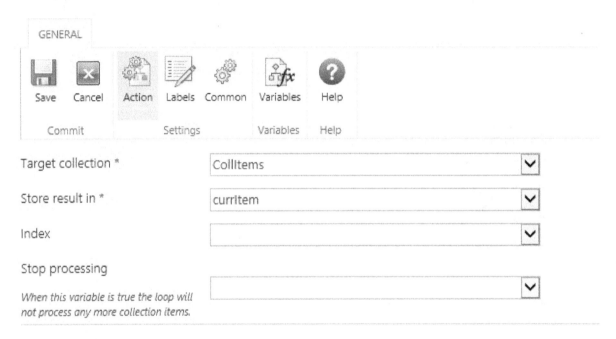

- The actions inside the **For each** will be repeated
- Drag a '**Set Variable**' action inside the '**For Each**' action

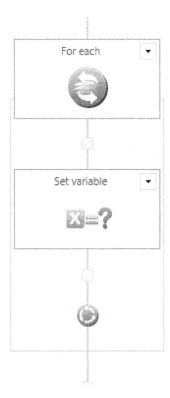

- Open the '**Set Variable**' action configuration page
- Set the '**SiteName**' variable for the current list item in the collection using the lookup values as defined below

Configure Action - Set variable

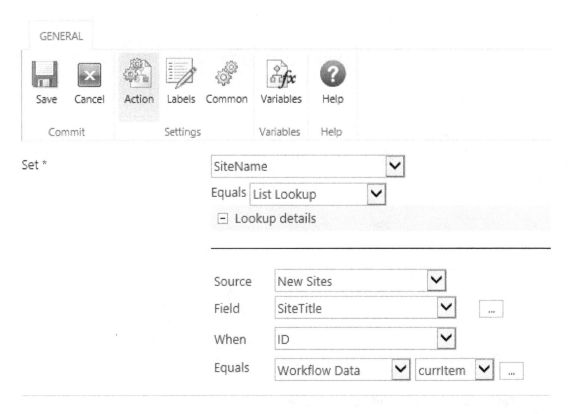

- Drag a second '**Set Variable**' action under the first

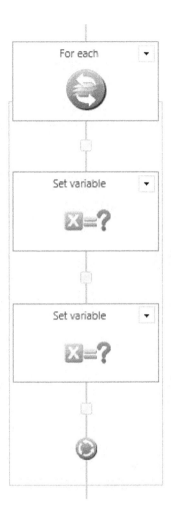

- Open the 'Set Variable' action configuration page
- Set the 'SiteURL' variable for the current list item in the collection using the lookup values as defined below

Configure Action - Set variable

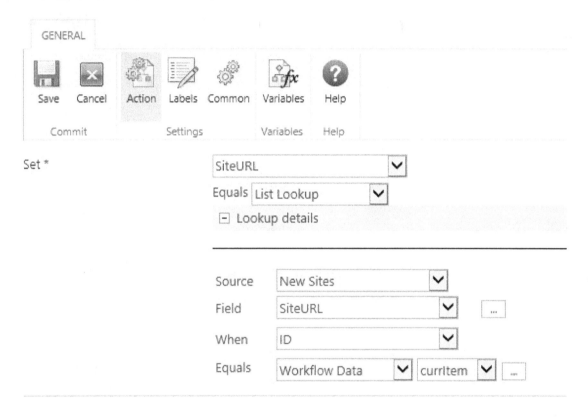

- Drag a 'Create Site' workflow action under the second 'Set Variable' action

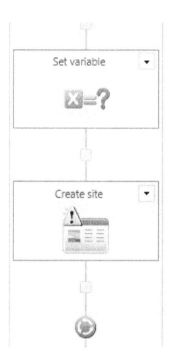

- Open the '**Create Site**' action **configuration** page
- Using the '**Insert Reference**' icon to the right of the Title box select the **SiteName** workflow variable
- Using the '**Insert Reference**' icon to the right of the URL name box select the **SiteURL** workflow variable
- Choose the '**Team Site**' template
- Enter your **credentials**

Configure Action - Create site

GENERAL

Save	Cancel	Action	Labels	Common	Variables	Help
Commit		Settings			Variables	Help

Title *   SiteName

Description

Inherit permissions   ☑

Parent site *   ● Select a parent site ○ Enter a URL

                            Nintex Demo ⬈

URL name *   SiteURL

Template *   Team Site ▼

Display on the Quick Launch of
the parent site   ☑

Display on the top link bar of the
parent site   ☐

Use top link bar from the parent
site   ☑

Store URL in   ▼

⊟ Override credentials

Credentials   Username v2013\mikem   🔒
                            Password •••••••••

- Save the 'Create Site' action

- **Save** and **Publish** the workflow

- To schedule the workflow on the 'Gear' menu click Nintex Workflow 2013 >> Schedule Site Workflows

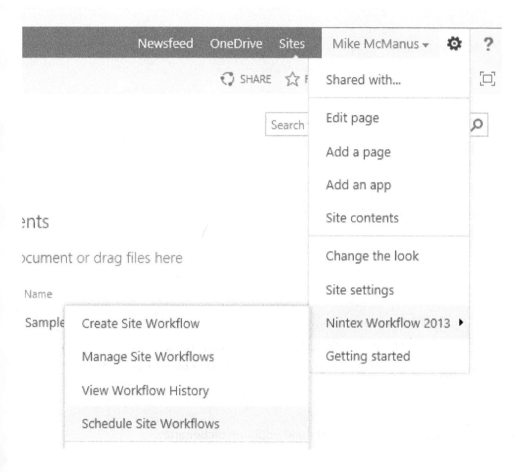

- Click 'Add Schedule'

- On the New Workflow Schedule page select the 'Create New Sites' workflow and choose a time in the next few minutes to start. Also indicate that the schedule should repeat daily

New Workflow Schedule

Create a new workflow schedule for a site workflow.

Workflow

Select a workflow for this schedule:	Create New Sites ▾

Schedule start

Start time	3/31/2015 🗓 11 AM ▾ 00 ▾

Repeat settings

Repeat every	1	Days ▾
Workdays only	☐	
If a repetition falls on a non-workday, it waits until the next workday to run.		

Schedule End

⦿ Date	3/31/2015 🗓 12 PM ▾ 00 ▾
○ Number of repeats	0
○ Indefinite	

Start Data

Dictionaries

Dictionaries are very similar in use to collections. Collections are not available in Nintex Workflow for Office 365, but Dictionaries are. Think of a dictionary variable as a group of name / value pairs.

The 'Build Dictionary' workflow action is used to create and populate dictionaries.

The 'Get an Item From a Dictionary' workflow action is used to retrieve values from a dictionary variable.

Demo 8 - Using a Site Workflow and Dictionary to Loop in Office 365

Site workflows are not tied to a specific library or list. In this exercise we will create a workflow to automate the process of looping through multiple list items and acting on each. A dictionary stores multiple values, similar to an array. In this exercise we will query list items that meet a certain criteria and then send an email for each item and update the item as having been processed.

This is very similar to the Collections and Looping demonstration, and is a good alternative to Collection variables when working in Office 365 / SharePoint online.

- On the Gear icon click **Add an App**

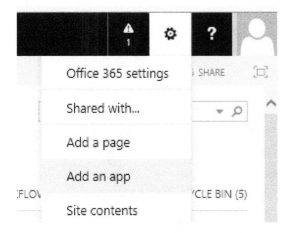

- On the Your Apps page click **Custom List**

Document Library
Popular built-in app
App Details

Custom List
Popular built-in app
App Details

Tasks
Popular built-in app
App Details

Site Mailbox
Popular built-in app
App Details

- Name the new Custom List *YourName_SiteRequests*

- Click the new list name to navigate to the list

- On the **List** tab of the ribbon click **List Settings**

- On the **List Settings** page scroll down under the columns section and click **Create Column.**

    Name the column *Requested Site Name*

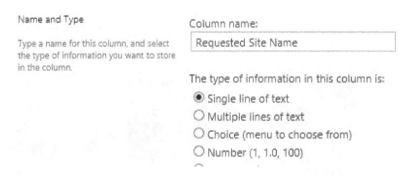

- On the **List Settings** page scroll down under the columns section and click **Create Column.**

    Name the column *Requested Site URL*

Settings › Create Column ⓘ

Name and Type

Type a name for this column, and select the type of information you want to store in the column.

Column name:

Requested Site URL

The type of information in this column is:

◉ Single line of text
○ Multiple lines of text
○ Choice (menu to choose from)
○ Number (1, 1.0, 100)

- On the **List Settings** page scroll down under the columns section and click **Create Column.** Name the column *Completed.* Select Yes/No (check box) as the Type. Scroll down and select No as the Default and click **OK**

Settings › Create Column ⓘ

Name and Type

Type a name for this column, and select the type of information you want to store in the column.

Column name:

Completed

The type of information in this column is:

○ Single line of text
○ Multiple lines of text
○ Choice (menu to choose from)
○ Number (1, 1.0, 100)
○ Currency ($, ¥, €)
○ Date and Time
○ Lookup (information already on this site)
◉ Yes/No (check box)
○ Person or Group

- Site Workflows are created from the **Site Contents** page

- On the **Gear** icon click **Site Contents**

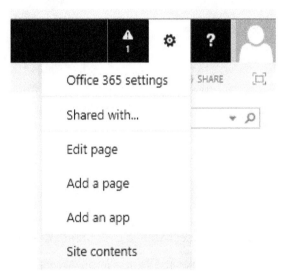

- On the **Site Contents** page click **Nintex Workflow for Office 365**

- When the Workflow Design canvas opens click **Settings** in the ribbon

- On the **Settings** page enter **YourName_SiteRequestsWF** as the **Name**. Select your WF Task list for the **Task List** and click **Save**

Name	YourName_SiteRequestsWF
Description	
Task list	MikeM_WF_Tasks ⌄
History list	Workflow History ⌄

- Click **Variables** in the ribbon. On the Variables page use the **New** button to create the following variables

Name	Type
ResultCount	Integer
FirstColumn	Dictionary
FieldsXML	Dictionary
OutFromDictionary	Text
CurrentIndex	Integer
ResultCountInner	Integer
FirstColumnInner	Dictionary
CurrentIndexInner	Number
FieldsXMLInner	Dictionary
SiteName	Text
SiteURL	Text

- Drag an Office 365 Query List action onto the design canvas

- Click the down arrow and click **Configure**

- On the Configure dialog for **Destination Site URL** click **Advanced Lookup** and select **Workflow Context** and **Current Site URL** and then click **Insert**

- On the Configure dialog for **List Name** type the name of your Site Requests list

- On the Configure dialog for **SharePoint Online URL** click **Advanced Lookup** and select **Workflow Context** and **Current Site URL** and then click **Insert**

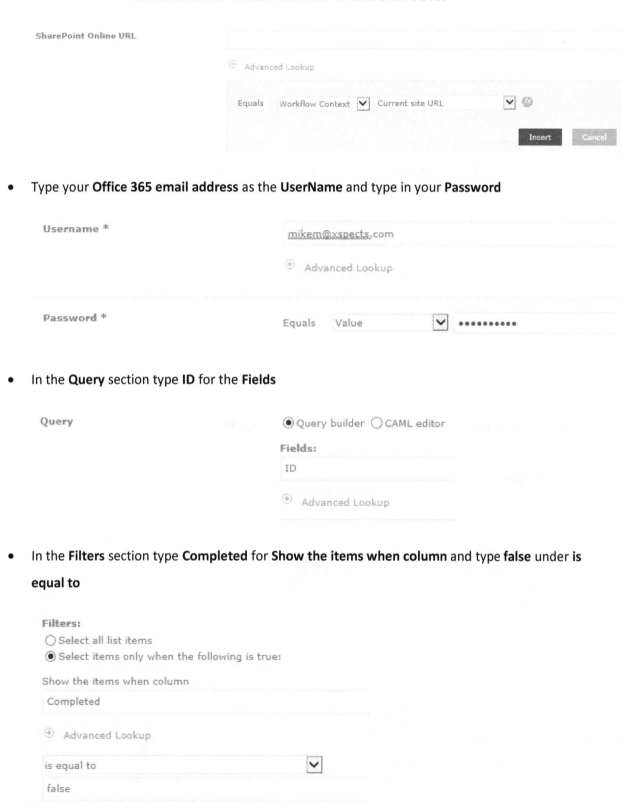

- Type your **Office 365 email address** as the **UserName** and type in your **Password**

- In the **Query** section type **ID** for the **Fields**

- In the **Filters** section type **Completed** for **Show the items when column** and type **false** under **is equal to**

- In the **Sort** section type **ID** under **First sort by column**

  Sort:

  First sort by column:

  ID

- Select workflow variables as below (note that **FirstColumn** is a dictionary variable!)

Result count	ResultCount
First column	FirstColumn
	First column value(s).
Fields XML	FieldsXML
	Collection of item metadata as XML.

- Drag a Set workflow variable action under the **Office 365 query list** action

- Click the down arrow and click **Configure**

- On the **Configure** dialog enter the values as below and click **Save**

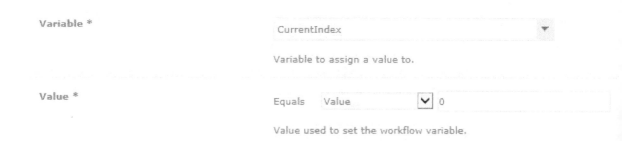

- Drag a **Loop N Times** action under the **Set Workflow Variable** action

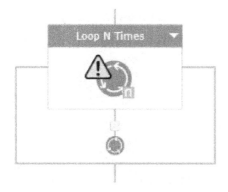

- Click the down arrow and click **Configure**

- On the **Configure** dialog enter the values as below and click **Save**

- Drag a **Get an Item from a Dictionary** inside the loop

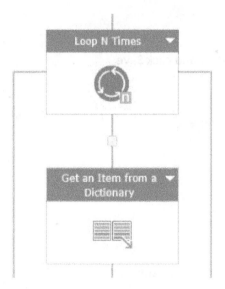

- Click the down arrow and click **Configure**

- On the **Configure** dialog for Item **Name or Path** click **Advanced Lookup** and then select the **CurrentIndex** variable, and click **Insert**

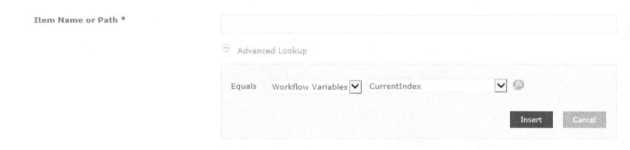

- After you click Insert you must manually wrap the variable in parentheses

({Variable:CurrentIndex})

- Select variables for **Dictionary** and **Output** as below and click **Save**

Dictionary *

FirstColumn

The dictionary variable to get the value from.

Output *

OutFromDictionary

Workflow variable output by this action.

- Drag an **Office 365 query list** action beneath the **Get an Item for a Dictionary action**

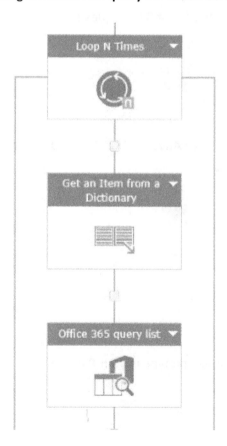

- Click the down arrow and click **Configure**
- On the Configure dialog for **Destination Site URL** click **Advanced Lookup** and select **Workflow Context** and **Current Site URL** and then click **Insert**

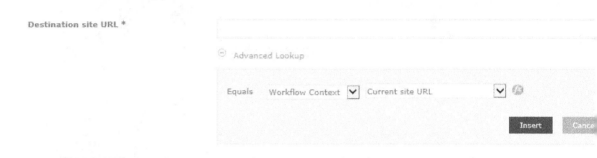

- On the Configure dialog for **List Name** type the name of your Site Requests list

- On the Configure dialog for **SharePoint Online URL** click **Advanced Lookup** and select **Workflow Context** and **Current Site URL** and then click **Insert**

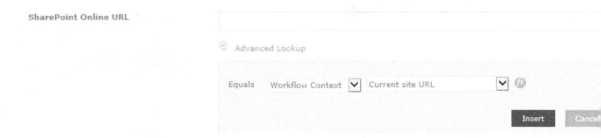

- Type your **Office 365 email address** as the **UserName** and type in your **Password**

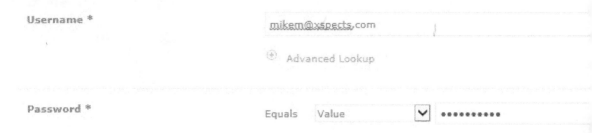

- In the **Query** section type **Requested Site Name** for the **Fields** value

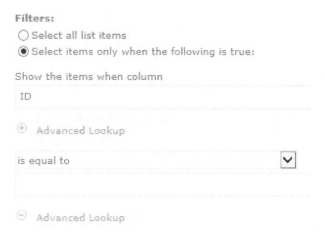

- In the **Filters** section type **ID** for **Show the items when column** and click **Advanced Lookup** under **is equal to**

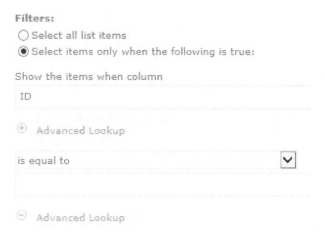

- In the **Advanced Lookup** section select the **OutFromDictionary** workflow variable

- In the **Sort** section type **ID** under **First sort by column**

- Select workflow variables as below (note that **FirstColumn** is a dictionary variable!)

- Click **Save**

- Drag a **Get an Item from a Dictionary** under the **Office 365 query list** action

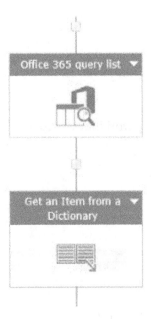

- Click the down arrow and click **Configure**

- On the **Configure** dialog for Item **Name or Path** type **(0)** and then select variables for **Dictionary** and **Output** as below and click **Save**

Item Name or Path *

(0)

Advanced Lookup

Name or path of the item (key) to get from the dictionary.

Dictionary *

FirstColumnInner

The dictionary variable to get the value from.

Output *

SiteName

Workflow variable output by this action.

- Drag an **Office 365 query list** action beneath the **Get an Item for a Dictionary action**

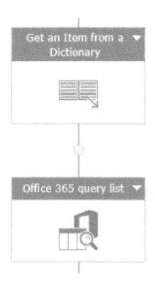

- Click the down arrow and click **Configure**

- On the Configure dialog for **Destination Site URL** click **Advanced Lookup** and select **Workflow Context** and **Current Site URL** and then click **Insert**

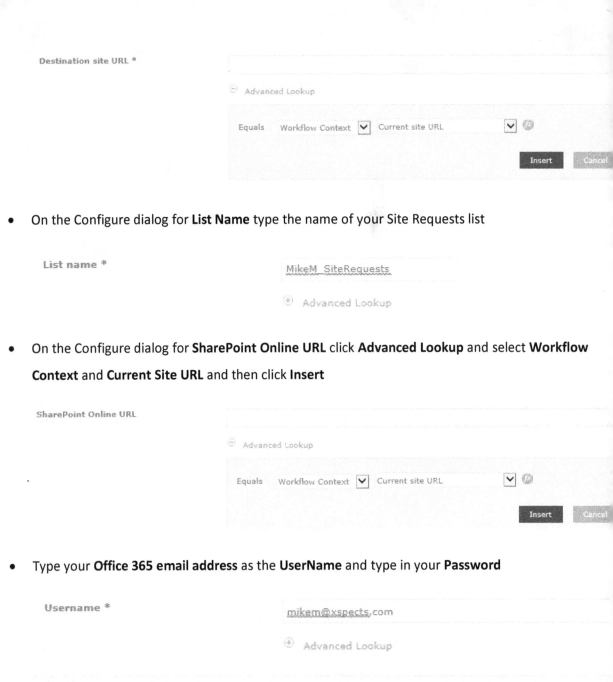

- On the Configure dialog for **List Name** type the name of your Site Requests list

- On the Configure dialog for **SharePoint Online URL** click **Advanced Lookup** and select **Workflow Context** and **Current Site URL** and then click **Insert**

- Type your **Office 365 email address** as the **UserName** and type in your **Password**

- In the **Query** section type **Requested Site URL** for the **Fields** value

- In the **Filters** section type **ID** for **Show the items when column** and click **Advanced Lookup** under **is equal to**

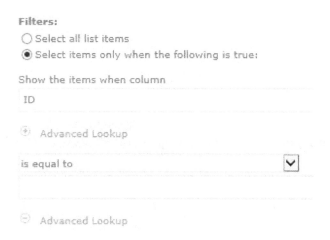

- In the **Advanced Lookup** section select the **OutFromDictionary** workflow variable

- In the **Sort** section type **ID** under **First sort by column**

- Select workflow variables as below (note that **FirstColumn** is a dictionary variable!)

- Click **Save**

- Drag a **Get an Item from a Dictionary** under the **Office 365 query list** action

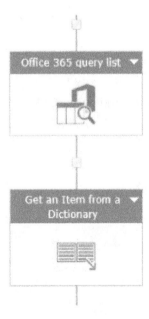

- Click the down arrow and click **Configure**

- On the **Configure** dialog for Item **Name or Path** type **(0)** and then select variables for **Dictionary** and **Output** as below and click **Save**

Item Name or Path *	(0)
	⊕ Advanced Lookup
	Name or path of the item (key) to get from the dictionary.
Dictionary *	FirstColumnInner ▼
	The dictionary variable to get the value from.
Output *	SiteURL ▼
	Workflow variable output by this action.

- Drag a **Set Workflow Variable** action under the **Get Item from a Dictionary** action

- Click the down arrow and click **Configure**

- On the **Configure** dialog input the values as below. For the Value field use the Advanced Lookup function to add the two values. Click **Save**

361

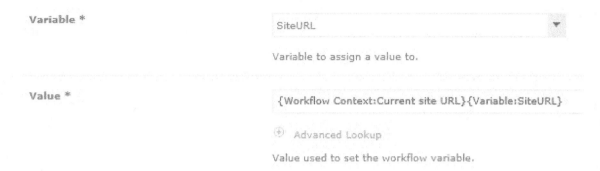

Variable *

SiteURL

Variable to assign a value to.

Value *

{Workflow Context:Current site URL}{Variable:SiteURL}

⊕ Advanced Lookup

Value used to set the workflow variable.

- Drag a **Do Calculation** action under the **Set Workflow Variable** action

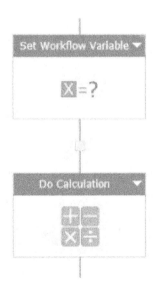

- Click the down arrow and click **Configure**

- On the **Configure** dialog input the values as below and click **Save**

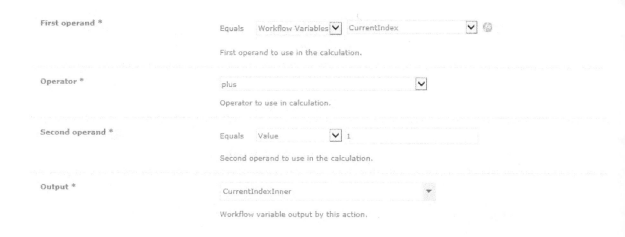

First operand *
Equals   Workflow Variables ⌄   CurrentIndex   ⌄

First operand to use in the calculation.

Operator *
plus   ⌄

Operator to use in calculation.

Second operand *
Equals   Value   ⌄   1

Second operand to use in the calculation.

Output *
CurrentIndexInner   ⌄

Workflow variable output by this action.

Save   Cancel

- Drag a **Set Workflow Variable** action under the **Do Calculation** action

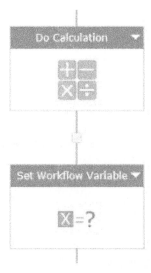

- Click the down arrow and click **Configure**
- On the **Configure** dialog input the values as below and click **Save**

- Drag a **Send an Email** action under the **Set Workflow Variable** action

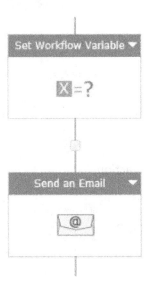

- Click the down arrow and click **Configure**

- On the **Configure** dialog enter your Email address as the **To** field and *New Site Request* as the **Subject**

- In the **Body** enter the following values (using the **Advanced Lookup** link to add the variables) and then click **Save**

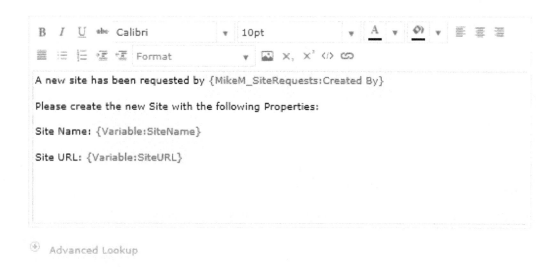

- Below is an example of the email as it is sent

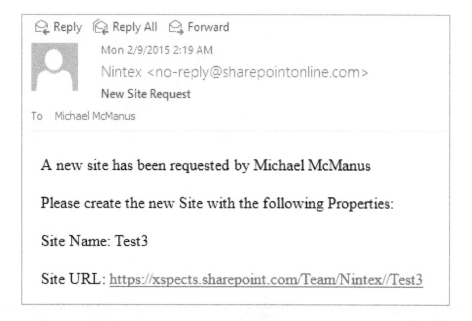

- Drag an **Update List Item** action under the **Send an Email** action

- Click the down arrow and click **Configure**

- On the **Configure** dialog enter the values as below and click **Save**

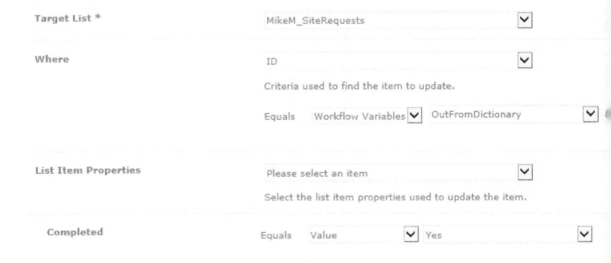

- **Save** and **Publish** the workflow

Demo 9 - Using an App Step to Run with Elevated Permissions

Nintex Workflow for Office 365 does not have an Action Set like on premises Nintex Workflow. Instead Nintex Workflow for Office 365 uses an App Step.

- On the Gear icon click **Site Contents**

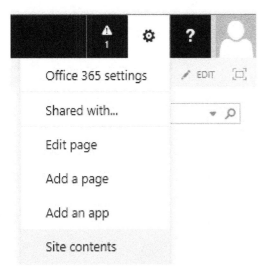

- On the **Site Contents** page click **Nintex Workflow for Office 365**

- When the Workflow Design canvas opens click **Open** in the ribbon

- Select the Workflow you created in the last exercise and click **Open**

- Drag an **App Step** action onto the workflow design canvas, just below the **Start** icon

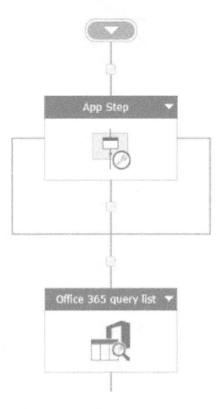

- Drag all of the other actions into the **App Step**
- **Save** and **Publish** the workflow

State Machines and States

The State Machine workflow action is a container. The State Machine contains other workflow actions. Within the State Machine workflow actions can be repeated and re-routed, to accommodate use cases such as re-submitting items for approval after being initially rejected.

We have seen a few different workflow actions that allow us to define multiple execution paths.

Switch, Run Parallel, Assign Flexi Task among others all present us with multiple execution paths.

The State Machine gives us the ability to not only build multiple execution paths, but to also jump back and forth between execution paths.

This can be helpful when we need the actions in one path to lead to actions in another path. State Machines allow us to not only jump between execution paths, they also allow us to repeat execution paths.

The individual execution paths in a State Machine are the States. Thus in a State Machine we control execution by switching the active State.

The State Machine can have multiple execution branches or States. Using the Change State workflow action State Machines re-direct execution to different execution branches. A State Machine usually has at least 2 states, but can have more.

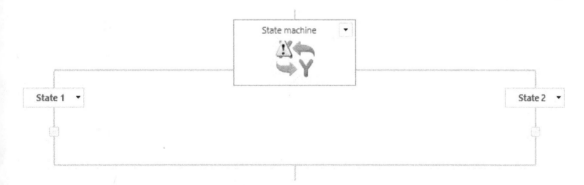

Note below that when you configure a State Machine you must select an Initial State

Configure Action - State machine

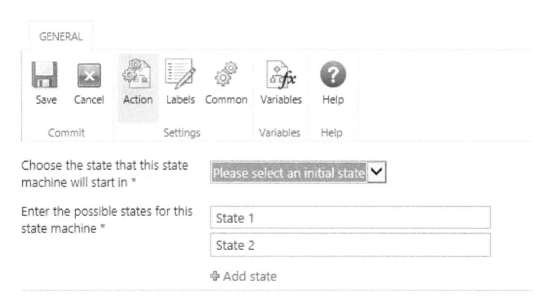

Demo 10 - States and State Machines

In this demonstration we will use a State Machine to control the flow of an approval requiring both multiple reviews and approvals, but also re-reviews.

The following workflow will provide the following functionality:

A document author will submit a document to a document library. The author's manager will be assigned a review and approve task. The manager can either Approve, Reject or Send Back for Changes.

If the manager 'Sends Back for Changes' the author will make changes and then 'Re-Submit' the document (within the same workflow, not as a second workflow).

After being re-submitted the manager repeats the process by either Approving, Rejecting or Sending Back for Changes.

This cycle will continue until either the Author chooses not to re-submit, or the manager either Approves or Rejects the document.

- Create a new Document Library called 'Submissions'
- On the Submissions document library ribbon click 'Create a Workflow in Nintex Workflow' under Workflow Settings

- Select the Blank workflow template and click Create

Select a Workflow Template   □ ✕

Blank

Business Management /
Finance

Human Resources

Operations and IT

Project Tracking / Product
Management

Sales / Marketing

Blank

Design a new workflow
from a blank page.
Alternatively, select a
template from one of the
categories.

Create   Cancel

- Click Workflow Settings

- On the **Workflow Settings** page name the workflow **Submit and Re Submit**
- Select **Yes** to start the workflow automatically when new items are created

Workflow Settings

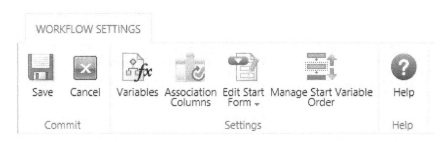

Title and description

Title *   Submit and Re Submit

Description

Workflow options

Start manually   ☑

Require manage list rights   ☐

Start when items are created   Yes ▼

Start when items are modified   No ▼

- **Save** the settings
- Drag a **State Machine** workflow action onto the design canvas
- Click the drop down arrow on the upper right of the **State Machine** action and click **Configure**

- Change the State names to **Submit** and **Review** as below and select **Review** as the initial state

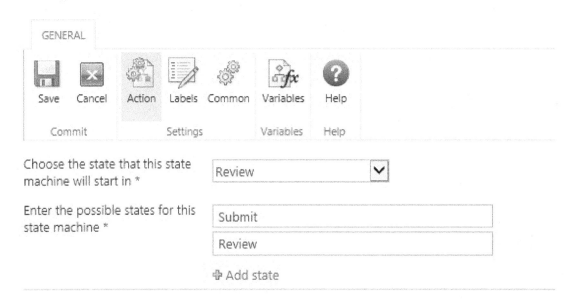

- **Save** the **State Machine** action

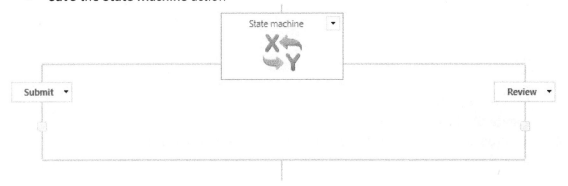

- Drag a **Flexi Task** action under the **Review** branch

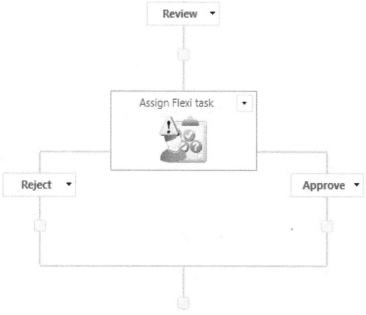

- Click the drop down arrow on the upper right of the **Flexi Task** action and click **Configure**

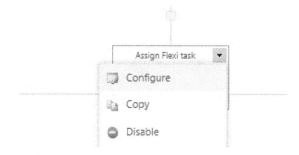

- On the **Configure Action** dialog click the address book icon to the right of the **Assignees** field

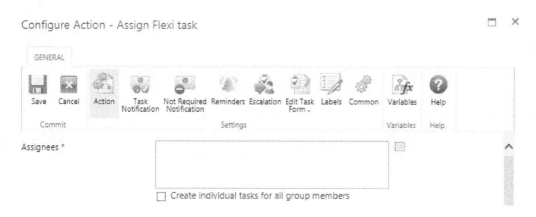

- On the **Select People and Groups** dialog click **Lookup** and then choose **Manager**

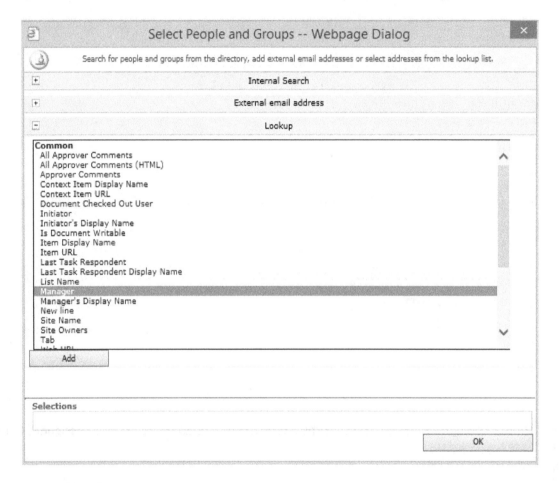

- Click **Add** and **OK**

- Save the **Assign Flexi Task** action

- Drag a **Change State** action under the **Reject** branch of the **Assign Flexi Task** action

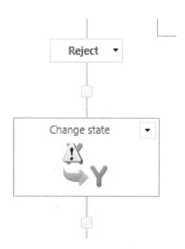

- Open the **Change State** action configuration page and select **Submit** as the **Next State**.
- In other words if the manager Rejects the submission it goes to the Submit execution branch or state

Configure Action - Change state

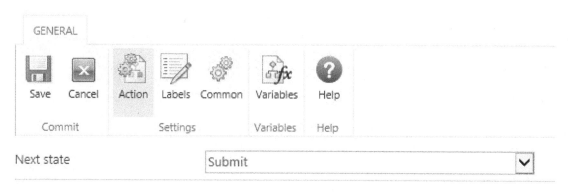

- **Save** the **Change State** action
- We could place a **Change State** action under the **Approve** branch but if we put nothing there the workflow will simply end, which is fine for this demonstration
- Drag an **Assign a To Do Task** under the **Submit** branch

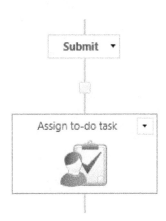

- Open the **Assign To Do Task** action configuration page
- On the **Configure Action** dialog click the address book icon to the right of the **Assignees** field

Configure Action - Assign to-do task

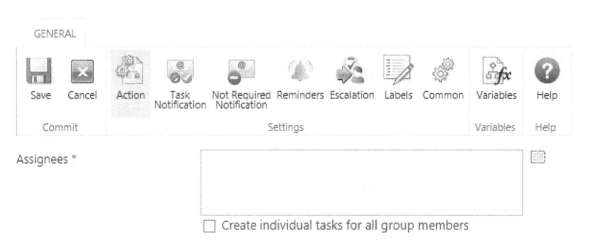

- On the **Select People and Groups** dialog click **Lookup** and then choose **Initiator**

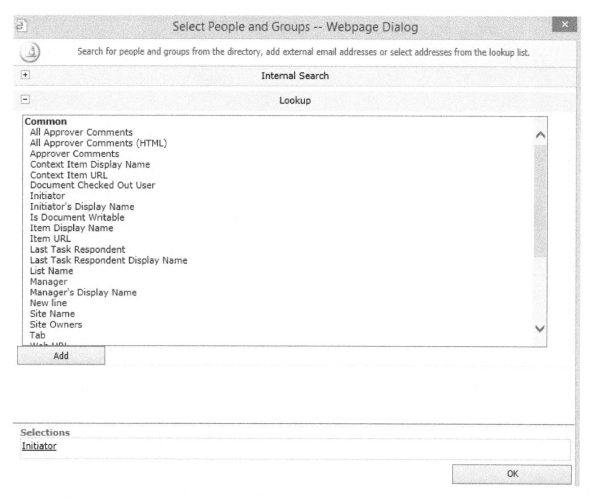

- Click **Add** and **OK**

Configure Action - Assign to-do task

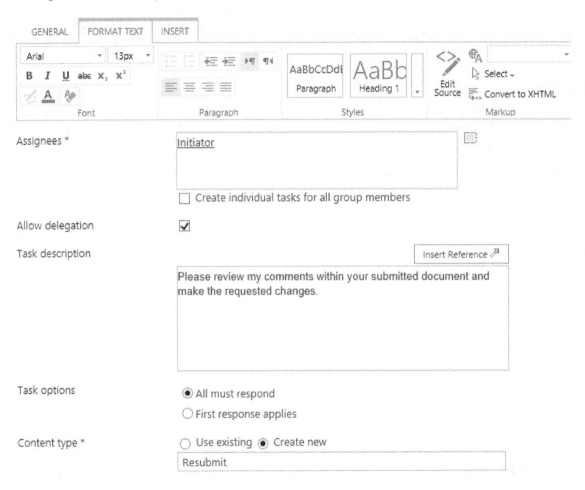

- **Save** the task
- Drag a **Change State** workflow action under the **Assign To Do Task** action

- Open the **Change State** action configuration page and select **Review** as the **Next State**

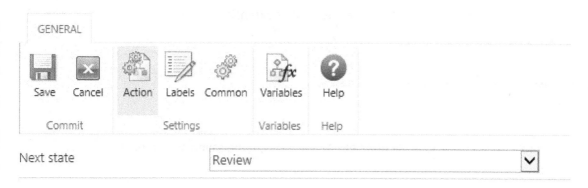

- **Save** the Change State action
- **Save** and **Publish** the workflow

This is a pretty simple State Machine, but by using multiple States, and even multiple State Machines it is easy to create very complex processes.

Re-Use

Workflow actions that have been configured can be saved for re-use. Even entire workflows can be saved for re-use.

Export/Import

Workflows can be exported and subsequently imported for re-use.

When a workflow is exported it is saved as a file with a .nwf extension.

An exported workflow can be imported into a new workflow.

Snippets

Workflow actions can be added to an Action Set. Action Sets can be saved as a snippet.

In the screenshot below the State Machine we created in the previous demonstration has been added to an Action Set

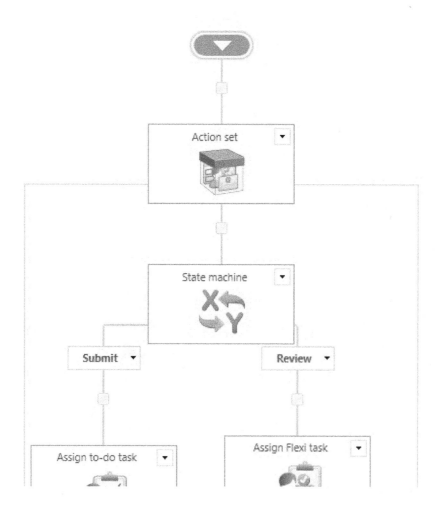

From the Action Set's menu can save the Action Set as a Snippet

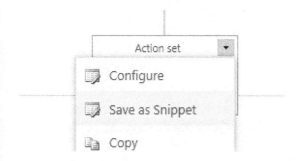

Save as Snippet

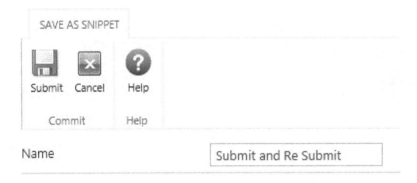

Once we have saved a snippet it is available to us in the My Snipptes section of the toolbox

My Snippets are available to you throughout the Nintex deployment, but they are limited to you. They are not shared with other users.

User Defined Actions

User Defined Actions are groups of Nintex Workflow Actions that have been configured and saved, and are available for re-use within the farm. User Defined Actions (UDAs) are very similar to snippets, except that UDAs are available to all users.

UDA Ribbon for the Farm

User Defined Actions can be scoped to either a single SharePoint Web, a Site Collection, or globally at the SharePoint Farm level.

Manage UDAs for a single SharePoint Web site from the site actions menu:

- On the site's homepage click Manage User Defined Actions on the Site Actions menu

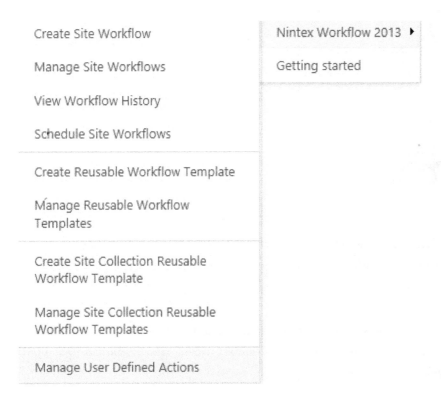

Manage UDAs for a Site Collection, click Manage User Defined Actions for the top level site in the site collection and click the link that says *Switch to the Site Collection Level Settings*

All User Defined Actions are created at the Site (single web) level. They can then be promoted to the Site Collection level. Note that the Create icon is only present on the ribbon at the Site level, it is not on the ribbon for either Site Collection UDAs or Farm UDAs.

Creating a User Defined Action is just like creating a new Workflow, except that instead of a Workflow Settings icon there is a UDA Settings icon

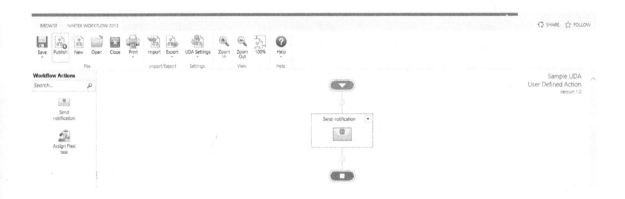

Demo 11 - Create a User Defined Action

User Defined Actions are like snippets, except that they can be re-used by all Nintex Workflow users, not just the author of the snippet.

In this demonstration we will create a User Defined Function UDA from the State Machine workflow we create earlier.

- On the **Submissions** library ribbon click **Manage Workflows with Nintex Workflow**

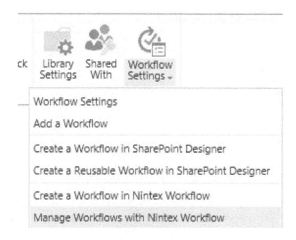

- Click the **Submit and Re Submit** workflow

Submissions ▸ Workflow Gallery ⓘ

🖥 Create

Published Workflows

Name	Modified By
Submit and Re Submit	Mike McManus

Unpublished Workflows

Name	Modified By

- Drag an **Action Set** onto the design canvas, above the **State Machine**

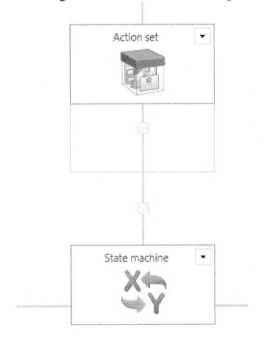

- **Minimize** the **State Machine**

- Drag the State Machine into the Action Set

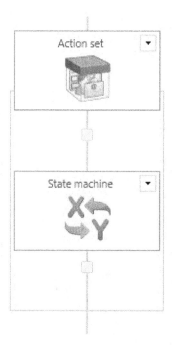

- Save the **Action Set** as a snippet

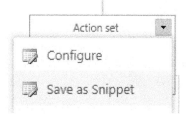

Save as Snippet

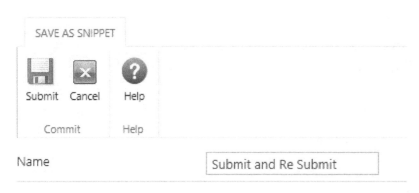

Name   Submit and Re Submit

- **Save** the snippet and confirm it shows in **My Snippets**

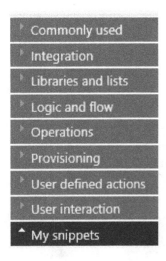

Submit and Re
Submit

- On the site's homepage click **Manage User Defined Actions** on the **Site Actions** menu

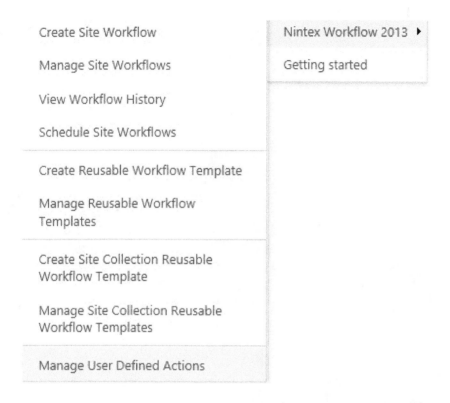

- On the **Manage User Defined Actions** page click **Create**

- Drag the **Submit and Re Submit** snippet onto the design canvas

Workflow Actions

Search... 🔍

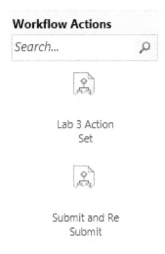

Lab 3 Action
Set

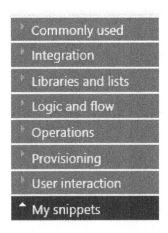

Submit and Re
Submit

▸ Commonly used

▸ Integration

▸ Libraries and lists

▸ Logic and flow

▸ Operations

▸ Provisioning

▸ User interaction

▲ My snippets

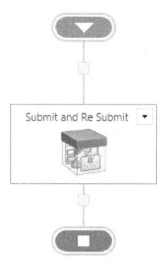

- **Maximize** the **Action Set** and you will see the entire **State Machine** workflow

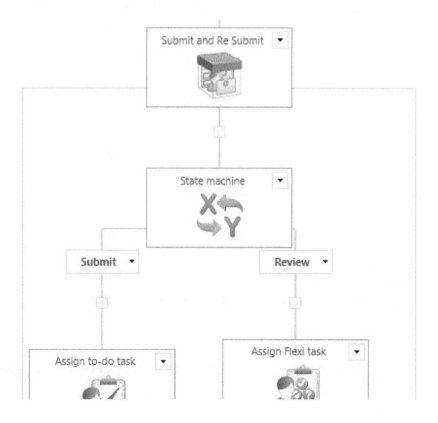

- Click **UDA Settings**

- On the **User Defined Actions Settings** page enter **Submit and Re Submit UDA** as the title

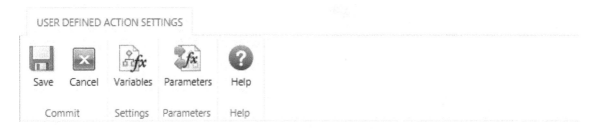

Title and description

Title *   Submit and Re Submit UDA

- **Save** and **Publish** the User Defined Action
- Your workflow actions panel now includes this (and another UDAs you have made)

Installation and Configuration

Before use Nintex Workflow for SharePoint 2013 on premises must first be installed and configured.

- Installation of Nintex Workflow Installation files
  - o Install Nintex Workflow for SharePoint 2013 setup files. These setup files will install the Nintex Workflow Solutions to your SharePoint Farm.

Deploy Solutions

- o Within SharePoint 2013 Central Administration go to System Settings >> Manage Farm Solutions
- o Note - if you are installing both Nintex Workflow and Nintex Forms you must deploy the Nintex Workflow solutions first.

Solution Management ⓘ

Name

nintexforms2013.wsp

nintexforms2013backwardscompatibilityui.wsp

nintexforms2013core.wsp

nintexworkflow2013.wsp

nintexworkflow2013backwardscompatibilityui.wsp

nintexworkflow2013core.wsp

nintexworkflow2013enterprisefeatures.wsp

nintexworkflow2013enterprisefeaturesbackwardscompat.wsp

- o Deploy Nintex Solutions in this order:
  - Nintexworkflow2013core.wsp
  - Nintexworkflow2013.wsp
  - Nintexworkflow2013enterprisefeatures.wsp (if you have an Enterprise License)

After installation and deployment of Nintex Products there will be new options in both Central Administration and with the Site Settings pages for Site Collections using the Nintex products.

The following sections are added left navigation in SharePoint Central Administration:

- Nintex Workflow Management
- Nintex Forms Management

Central Administration

Application
Management

System Settings

Monitoring

Backup and Restore

Security

Upgrade and Migration

General Application
Settings

Apps

Office 365

Nintex Workflow
Management

Nintex Forms
Management

Configuration Wizards

The Nintex Workflow Management page in Central Administration has links to various configuration options:

Nintex Workflow Management

 Nintex Workflow Management
Licensing   Database setup   Web Application activation   Manage allowed actions   Global settings
LazyApproval settings   Message templates   Manage workflow constants   Manage user defined actions
Manage context data   Manage holidays   Manage workflow reports   Administration reports
Workflow error notifications   Purge workflow data   Support console   Live settings   Live catalog settings

Configuration

- o Licensing - For full functionality you must import the license file provided by Nintex
  - On the Central Administration Home page click Nintex Workflow Management
  - click Licensing
  - click Import
  - Browse to locate your license file and then click Import
  - Click OK
- o Database setup - You must create at least one Nintex Content Database
  - On the Central Administration Home page click Nintex Workflow Management
  - Click Database setup
  - Click Create in the Configuration Database section
  - Enter the Name of your database server and database name
  - Click OK
  - Execute an IISRESET
- o Web Application Activation - Define which SharePoint web applications have Nintex Features activated.
- o Manage Allowed Actions - Define which Workflow Actions are available within SharePoint site collections

* Note the following settings should all be reviewed and set/adjusted as needed.

- o Global Settings - Define global configuration settings
  - Email Settings

Outbound SMTP Server:

SampleSMTPServer

☐ SMTP server requires authentication
Username:

Password:

From Address:

nintex@xspects.com

Reply To Address:

nintex@xspects.com

Character Set:

65001 (Unicode UTF-8) ⌄

☐ Specify different encoding for plain text emails
65001 (Unicode UTF-8) ⌄

☐ Specify different encoding for SMS messages
65001 (Unicode UTF-8) ⌄

Use css styles in HTML emails:

○ Yes ◉ No

Location of stylesheet containing email styles:

/_layouts/ NintexWorkflow/htmleditorstyles.css

- Instant Messaging Settings
- Enforce Safe Looping
  - This option demands workflow actions are marked as allowed at run time. A running workflow will error if an action which is not 'allowed' is executed.
- Allow the Execute SQL action to impersonate the application pool identity
- Allow workflow schedules to impersonate the system account
- Allow sending notifications on behalf of another user
- Allow 'Run now' on actions that interact with external data
- Allow verbose workflow logging
- Enforce message header and footer
- Specify a default task list name
- Long term delegation
- Site administrators long term delegation
- Notification preferences

- Workflow schedule permissions
- Task form properties view
- Default workflow start page
- Default task edit page
- Default task view page
- Default task edit page for Flexi tasks
- Default task view page for Flexi tasks
- Workflow statistics permissions
  - Lazy Approval Settings
    - Enable/Disable Lazy Approval
    - Edit the Lazy Approval Footer
    - Create and Manage Lazy Approval Terms

The phrase or terms used by the Lazy Approval are the words that can be sent in an email reply. You can add new terms and map them to the appropriate outcome. For example you could add a term/phrase 'Roger' and map it Approve as an outcome.

The Lazy Approval will be available to the following Actions:

- Assign Flexi Task
- Request Approval
- Request Review
- Request Data

The table below shows the out of the box or default Lazy Approval terms/phrases

Phrase	Outcome
approve	Approve
approved	Approve
decline	Deny
declined	Deny
no	Deny
ok	Approve
reject	Deny
rejected	Deny
yes	Approve

- o Message Templates
    - ▪ Message Templates define the look, feel and content of email messages generated by Nintex Workflows. These templates can be customized.
        - • Default Header Template - This header is added to all messages sent by Nintex Workflow

Notification Header

- • Default Approval Required Notification Template - These messages are sent whenever an Approval task is assigned.

Approval Required Notification

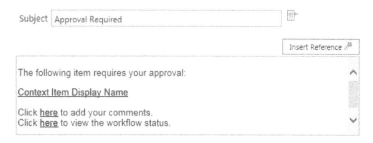

- • Default Approval No Longer Required Notification Template - These messages are sent if an Approval task has been assigned, but subsequently dealt with by another user.

Approval No Longer Required Notification

- • Notification Footer Template - This is added to the bottom of all messages sent by Nintex Workflow

Notification Footer

      ○   Manage Workflow Constants

Workflow Constants allow you to define values that will be available for use in workflows throughout the SharePoint Farm.

When you create a new Workflow Constant you must define:

- ○ Name
- ○ Type
    - ▪ String
    - ▪ Number
    - ▪ Date
    - ▪ Credential - Consists of:
        - • Username
        - • Password
        - • Secure String - A text value that can only be used in workflow action input fields that do not show the value to an end user. The value is also masked in the constant management screen. This constant data type is useful for security tokens used in Nintex Live enabled workflow actions.
- ○ Value
- ○ Description

- o Sensitive (Y/N) - If selected the value will not be displayed

Name *

Type   String

Value *

Description

Sensitive   ☐

*Selecting this option will restrict any
workflow from displaying the content of
the constant.*

- o Manage User Defined Actions

User Defined Actions are groups of Nintex Workflow Actions that have been configured and saved, and are available for re-use within the farm. User Defined Actions (UDAs) are very similar to snippets, except that UDAs are available to all users.

Within the User Defined Actions page in Central Administration you can only Import, Delete, Export or Analyze UDAs.

BROWSE   MANAGE USER DEFINED ACTIONS

Delete   Import   Export   Analyze   Help

        Manage   Help   *UDA Ribbon for the Farm*

User Defined Actions can be scoped to either a single SharePoint Web, a Site Collection, or globally at the SharePoint Farm level.

All User Defined Actions are created at the Site (single web) level. They can then be promoted to the Site Collection level. Note that the Create icon is only present on the ribbon at the Site level, it is not on the ribbon for either Site Collection UDAs or Farm UDAs.

- o   **Manage Context Data**

Allows you to modify existing context data and create new context data. Context Data is available for use within workflows from the Insert Reference interface

Nintex Workflow Management · Manage Context Data

Add new Context Data

Display Name	Description	Type	Assembly	Field Type
All Approver Comments	All comments made by all approvers in all task actions that have run in the workflow.	Nintex.Workflow.ContextDataItems.AllApproverComments	Nintex.Workflow, Version=1.0.0.0, Culture=neutral, PublicKeyToken=913f6bae0ca5ae12	Text
All Approver Comments (HTML)	All comments made by all approvers in all task actions that have run in the workflow, formatted for HTML.	Nintex.Workflow.ContextDataItems.AllApproverCommentsHtml	Nintex.Workflow, Version=1.0.0.0, Culture=neutral, PublicKeyToken=913f6bae0ca5ae12	Text
Approver Comments	The comments of the approvers who responded to the most recent task.	Nintex.Workflow.ContextDataItems.LastApproverComments	Nintex.Workflow, Version=1.0.0.0, Culture=neutral,	Text

- o   **Manage Holidays**
- o   **Manage Workflow Reports**

Nintex Workflow comes with reports that allow you to monitor Nintex Workflow Usage and Performance. In addition to managing existing reports (enabling and disabling) you can add new reports.

Title	Description
Approver Performance Statistics (all sites)	Use this report to view a list of workflow approvers and the total number of workflow tasks ass...
Completed Workflows (all sites)	Use this report to view all completed workflows, the initiator, start time, end time and total ...
Errored Workflows (all sites)	Use this report to view all workflows that have stopped due to error, the initiator, start time...
12 Month Usage Summary (all sites)	Use this report to view the total number of workflows started per month over the past 12 months...
30 Day Usage Summary (all sites)	Use this report to view the total number of workflows started per day over the past 30 days.
3 Month Usage Summary (all sites)	Use this report to view the total number of workflows started per week during the last 3 months...
Workflow Performance (all sites)	Use this report to view a list of all workflows and the total number started, in progress and t...
Workflows By Site	Use this report to view all sites with active workflows and the total completed, in progress, c...
Workflows In Progress (all sites)	Use this report to view all workflows in progress, the initiator, start time, last action date,...
Approver Performance Statistics	Use this report to view a list of workflow approvers, their average response time and the total...
Completed Workflows	Use this report to view all completed workflows, the initiator, start time, end time and total ...
Errored Workflows	Use this report to view all workflows that have stopped due to error, the initiator, start time...
12 Month Usage Summary	Use this report to view the total number of workflows started per month over the past 12 months...
30 Day Usage Summary	Use this report to view the total number of workflows started per day over the past 30 days.
3 Month Usage Summary	Use this report to view the total number of workflows started per week during the last 3 months...
Workflow Actions	Use this report to display all workflow actions within a workflow, the total number of instance...
Workflow Performance	Use this report to view a list of all workflows and the total number started, in progress and t...
Workflows In Progress	Use this report to view all workflows in progress, the initiator, start time, last action date,...
Overdue Workflows (all sites)	Use this report to view all workflows that have exceeded their expected duration for the curren...
Overdue Workflows	Use this report to view all workflows that have exceeded their expected duration for the curren...

- o   Administration Reports
- o   Workflow Error Notifications
- o   Purge Workflow Data
- o   Support Console

The Nintex Workflow Support Console provides a centralized location to view workflow errors from across your SharePoint deployment.

- o   Live Settings
- o   Live Catalog Settings

The following Site Collection Features are available within the Farm:

- Nintex Workflow 2013
- Nintex Workflow 2013 InfoPath Forms
- Nintex Workflow 2013 Reporting Web Parts
- Nintex Workflow 2013 Web Parts
- Nintex Workflow - Nintex Live Catalog

- Nintex Forms for Nintex Workflow
- Nintex Forms for SharePoint List Forms
- Nintex Forms Prerequisites Feature
- Nintex Live Forms

Nintex Forms for Nintex Workflow

Allow Nintex Workflow in this site collection to utilize Nintex Forms features.

Nintex Forms for SharePoint List Forms

Allow SharePoint lists and libraries in this site collection to utilize Nintex Forms features.

Nintex Forms Prerequisites Feature

The core SharePoint components for Nintex Forms to run within the site collection.

Nintex Live Forms

Allows Nintex Forms designers to publish the form to Nintex Live.

Nintex Workflow - Nintex Live Catalog

Allows Nintex Workflow designers to browse the Nintex Live Catalog.

Nintex Workflow 2013

Allow team sites in this site collection to utilize Nintex Workflow features.

Nintex Workflow 2013 InfoPath Forms

Allows Nintex Workflow to use start forms and task forms designed with Microsoft InfoPath.

Nintex Workflow 2013 Reporting Web Parts

Allows the Nintex Workflow Enterprise reporting web parts to be added to sites in this site collection.

Nintex Workflow 2013 Web Parts

Allows the Nintex Workflow web parts to be added to sites in this site collection.

The following configuration options are available within the Site Settings page (for top level sites in Site Collections using the Nintex Features)

Nintex Workflow
Workflows gallery
Message templates
Workflow templates
Allowed workflow designers
LazyApproval settings
Manage workflow constants
Scheduled workflows
Manage allowed actions
Manage holidays
Workflow change approval
Manage workflow history lists
Manage User Defined Actions
Workflow error notifications
Purge workflow data

For each site that will use Nintex Workflow you need to activate the appropriate Nintex Features. This independence at the site level from the Site Collection activation provides more flexibility for using Nintex products on some sites and not others.

Nintex Workflow 2013

Allows team sites in this site collection to utilize Nintex Workflow features.

Nintex Workflow 2013 Enterprise Reporting

Enables the use of Nintex Workflow 2013 Enterprise Reporting on this site.

www.ingramcontent.com/pod-product-compliance
Lightning Source LLC
Chambersburg PA
CBHW081505050326

40690CB00015B/2927